Praise for *Paths of*

Paths of the Righteous comes at a time when the Jewish people are under attack for daring to still be here after thousands of years of being hated, assimilated, or both. Read here how Olga Washington refuses to let uninformed antisemites decry Israel as apartheid, how Father Patrick Desbois repudiates those who would deny the Holocaust with his painstaking work, how Chloe Valdary combats unthinking bias through empathy and an unyielding determination to connect with people rather than make them feel scorned. These and their colleagues are the heroes we need in the twenty-first century, and I'm grateful to Ari Mittleman for telling their story.

Elisha Wiesel

Ari Mittleman's *Path of the Righteous* could not come at a better time. As we struggle to emerge from a global pandemic and deal with the ever-worsening climatic events that threaten our human existence, we are faced with a frightening and dramatic rise in global antisemitism, which has threatened the Jewish people's existence for millennia. The testimonies of the righteous non-Jews in Ari's book are a reminder that no minority group secures its basic rights and thrives without help from allies outside the group. The stories are also a reminder that it is incumbent upon us all to do better: to try to build bridges of understanding, compassion, and action to make our world a safer, more equitable, and brighter place.

S. Fitzgerald Haney, former U.S. Ambassador

Shakespeare wrote: "The evil that men do lives after them; The good is oft interred with their bones." Too often, Shakespeare's insight is true. Ari Mittleman corrects this moral imbalance. He's written an amazing, powerful, and gripping book about eight non-Jewish men and women who went above and beyond for the Jewish people. An altogether uplifting book.

Donna Brazile, Former Chairwoman, Democratic National Committee

Ari Mittleman has masterfully conveyed the stories and personalities of eight unique non-Jews who have spread their light to the Jewish people and to humanity as paradigms of decency, morality, and kindness. Ari paints the picture of their lives in a way that brings the reader into a different universe. After reading this incredible book, we are inspired, educated, and challenged to see hope and optimism in humanity knowing that there are refined, moral, and courageous people of all backgrounds who are willing to stand up against the world to do what is correct, fair, and righteous.

Rabbi Steven Weil, CEO, Friends of the Israel Defense Forces

In today's world, too often the focus is on division and difference. As a diplomat, I always try to look for common ground and to focus on the future and not dwell on the past. In an increasingly complex world, Mittleman's book strikes an optimistic tone with a creative and unique perspective.

Ambassador Ishmael Khaldi,
author, *A Shepherd's Journey: The Story of Israel's First Bedouin Diplomat*

Too often we are quick to condemn evil and slow to recognize righteousness. Ari Mittleman's eloquent book portrays remarkable people whose spirit, insight, and passion are powerful inspirations to improve ourselves and our world.

Rabbi David Wolpe, Sinai Temple, Los Angeles

With the understandable increase in anxiety about the return of antisemitism in our time, it is comforting and inspiring to read Ari Mittleman's stories of eight leaders who have taken the path of righteousness and harmony in the twenty-first century. In this book, Ari makes the case not to ignore persistent antisemitism but to be optimistic that people of good will can act together to defeat bigotry.

Senator Joseph I. Lieberman

At a time when Jews are extremely concerned and hurt due to rising antisemitism, we are gratified to hear every voice coming from our non-Jewish friends and allies who have been willing to stand with Israel and the Jewish people. Each voice becomes a gift that provides comfort and inspiration during difficult times. Jews need look no further than the powerful pages of this book to find love for Israel and the Jewish people expressed so profoundly by Ari Mittleman as he tells the stories of eight special non-Jewish righteous souls. Through the humanity and goodness of these eight beautiful people, we are infused with courage and hope.

Roz Rothstein, CEO, StandWithUs

Jewish tradition teaches us that the world exists because of thirty-six righteous human beings whom we do not necessarily know. Ari Mittleman reveals eight of those non-Jews who are righteous. Read *Paths of the Righteous* to be inspired. I survived because of a Catholic woman who risked her life in Poland to save me during the Shoah. Especially in these times, this book is a dose of optimism.

Abraham Foxman

We are given the choice, every day, whether we want our lives to be ordinary or whether we want them to be extraordinary. This book illuminates the moments and experiences that drove eight "normal" people to make an extraordinary impact. These eight stories of righteousness, integrity, and personal risk should inspire us all – and remind us, as Jews, that even in our darkest moments, we are never alone.

Amanda Berman, Founder and Executive Director, Zioness Movement

At a time when darkness seems to be growing and hatred is at epidemic proportions, Ari Mittleman has provided a ray of light and hope in *Paths of the Righteous*. These stories of eight honest and good people, who saw a need and sought to meet it, are inspiring because they are just the tip of the iceberg. There are many millions of such good-hearted people around the world who oppose antisemitism, admire the Jewish people, and love what Israel stands for. My prayer is that more of them will learn how to step up to the plate as did these brave individuals and have a greater impact on our world.

Dr. Susan Michael,
USA Director, International Christian Embassy Jerusalem

I am a child of the civil rights movement. I learned the importance of diverse allies from a young age. The Jewish community was there hand in hand with the African American community during the civil rights movement. Whether in the American South or the Middle East, everyone should be able to live in peace and coexist together. Ari Mittleman's *Paths of the Righteous* eloquently profiles diverse unheralded leaders working toward social justice, coexistence, and peace for Israel and the Jewish people.

Bakari Sellers, author, *My Vanishing Country*

Ari Mittleman was moved to write *Paths of the Righteous* after the devastating 2018 attack on the Tree of Life Synagogue in Pittsburgh. This book is a moving and hopeful response to that tragedy. *Paths of the Righteous* showcases the stories of eight men and women outside the Jewish tradition, people of varied nationalities and races, who boldly put their affinity for Israel and their allegiance with the Jewish people into action in their own communities. Their stories teach valuable and inspiring lessons about building bridges and standing up for what is right against all odds and shine a light of hope and humanity into a world that sometimes seems to be filled only with darkness. This book confirms what I've seen firsthand through the work of the Fellowship – the Jewish people are not alone as we fight against antisemitism and work for a peaceful and secure Israel.

Yael Eckstein,
President and CEO, International Fellowship of Christians and Jews

With the ongoing increase of global antisemitism, Ari Mittleman eloquently captures eight hopeful leaders who represent more of what unites us than what divides us. Fighting racism and bigotry means fighting all forms of it – especially antisemitism. Knowing we are not alone in this battle is critical.

Dr. Asaf Romirowsky,
Executive Director, Scholars for Peace in the Middle East

Ari Mittleman lifts up eight righteous leaders who have lifted others, eight unsung non-Jewish champions of the Jewish story, profiles in courage, defying the oldest hatred – antisemitism. Read these inspiring portraits for yourself and to your children; share with your colleagues, congregants, and friends. Mittleman reminds us, in lively prose, that a better day is not only possible, but already in motion.

Abigail Pogrebin,
author, *My Jewish Year: 18 Holidays, One Wondering Jew*

PATHS OF THE RIGHTEOUS

PATHS OF THE RIGHTEOUS

Stories of Heroism, Humanity, and Hope

ARI MITTLEMAN

gefen גפן
publishing house בית תרופות גפן Est. 1981
JERUSALEM ◆ NEW YORK

Cover Design: Cassandra Voors and Leah Ben Avraham/Noonim Graphics.
Typesetting: Optume Technologies

ISBN: 978-965-7023-73-0

1 3 5 7 9 8 6 4 2

Gefen Publishing House Ltd.
6 Hatzvi Street
Jerusalem 9438614,
Israel
972-2-538-0247
orders@gefenpublishing.com

Gefen Books
c/o Baker & Taylor Publisher Services
30 Amberwood Parkway
Ashland, Ohio 44805
516-593-1234
orders@gefenpublishing.com

www.gefenpublishing.com

Printed in Israel
Library of Congress Control Number: 2021909740

עֹז-וְהָדָר לְבוּשָׁהּ; וַתִּשְׂחַק, לְיוֹם אַחֲרוֹן
She is robed in strength and dignity;
and she smiles at the future.
(Proverbs 31:25)

For my daughter, Eliora
For her mother, Tova
For her grandmother, Elisheva, of blessed memory

Contents

אוֹר זָרֻעַ לַצַּדִּיק; וּלְיִשְׁרֵי לֵב שִׂמְחָה

Light is sown for the righteous, and joy for the upright in heart.
(Psalms 97:11)

לַיְּהוּדִים הָיְתָה אוֹרָה וְשִׂמְחָה

The Jews enjoyed light and joy.
(Esther 8:16)

Jewish sages over the centuries have devoted countless pages of commentary to these two lines. The consensus: light is mentioned before joy. Therefore, Jewish tradition teaches that while joy must always be our goal, light is the means to achieve it.

Preface

עֵץ חַיִּים הִיא לַמַּחֲזִיקִים בָּהּ, וְתֹמְכֶיהָ מְאֻשָּׁר
It is a tree of life to those who hold tight to it. (Proverbs 3:18)

During my walk to synagogue on the last Saturday of October 2018, I repeated the verse from Proverbs about Torah being a tree of life. I found myself humming the tune my parents had taught me as a boy to accompany it as my recently shined shoes met wet leaves. I laughed. I might be holding on tight to our tradition, I thought, but that tree was not holding on to its leaves as the wind picked up. By nightfall, the whole world would be familiar with the Jewish expression "tree of life," for just before lunchtime that Saturday, the Jewish day of rest, the Tree of Life congregation in the heart of Pittsburgh was attacked. A domestic terrorist with an assault rifle killed eleven worshipers and wounded six others.

Suburban Maryland is my adopted home, but Pennsylvania will always be my true home. Although I grew up several hundred miles away in Allentown, I've regularly visited with the Jewish community in Pittsburgh for work obligations. While we have strong differing opinions about the Flyers and the Penguins, what unites us is our faith and our love for Israel.

For days after the shooting, the news continued replaying images from the intersection of Wilkins and Shady. For me, the faces of the community members, the government leaders, their spouses, and their aides did not need a chyron. These were friends who joined me on the dance floor at my wedding. Others had traveled to Israel with me, and some provided homecooked meals after long cross-state drives.

Maybe it was the upcoming midterm election, but the political and social unrest seemed amplified, and I was reminded of the values my parents instilled in me at a young age: unity, bipartisanship, and patriotism. They fostered my love of history and geography, while teaching me how lucky I was to be an American, a country based on e pluribus unum: out of many, one.

xv

My father, a proud son of Rhode Island, instilled in me the values of religious pluralism and liberty that President George Washington shared on a humid August visit to the state in 1790, where he addressed the leaders of the first synagogue in the new country.

It was these values that led me to study and work with bipartisan leaders in our nation's capital, advocating for causes near and dear to my heart. Living in Maryland and working in Washington, DC, has provided me the chance to regularly attend meetings and events that have fortified the unbreakable bond between the United States and Israel. Professionally, I have been fortunate enough to travel the world, working with and learning from diverse leaders – presidents, prime ministers, monarchs, celebrities, business leaders, even a Nobel Peace Prize winner. Yet the individuals who are not household names and are seldom in the headlines intrigue me most. They are committed and passionate leaders in their own communities and fields, and I have learned from each of them just as much as the esteemed others.

The Babylonian Talmud teaches in *Kiddushin* 50a, "*Devarim she'ba'lev einam devarim*" (Words in the heart [words left unsaid] are irrelevant words). Thus, to grapple with the sleepless, emotional nights after the massacre in Pittsburgh, I felt compelled to craft an op-ed for my hometown newspaper in Allentown.

My parents, both academics, readily served as my editors and often encouraged me to follow Talmudic wisdom by committing pen to paper. I showed them the rough draft. My mother and I debated whether some positives could come from the worst antisemitic violence in American history. I was so focused on the bigger picture – how this would affect the historic midterm elections and what it meant to be a person of faith in an increasingly diverse and polarized America – that I never stopped to think about what might come next.

I didn't know it then, but on that Sunday night, I had the last meaningful conversation with my mother. Less than a month later, she died.

It was a cold, wet Black Friday that my wife, Tara, and I planned to spend in our pajamas. The day before had been an emotional roller coaster. We had driven six hours up to New Jersey and back to give thanks. We visited my wife's parents in a rehab facility where my father-in-law was recovering from a leg amputation and my mother-in-law from a stroke. We watched football, ate Chinese takeout, and were thankful that the worst appeared to be behind us.

Before dawn, my phone buzzed. When I finally picked up, my frantic father said my mother had died overnight, in the same chair in which she had helped me edit the op-ed column only three weeks prior.

I traveled alone to Pennsylvania that Friday afternoon. I arrived before sunset and, much to my surprise, my father had the table set for Shabbos dinner. Neither one of us had an appetite, nor could we remember a time when it had been just the two of us honoring the Sabbath.

Growing up, Friday nights were always sacred in our home. My parents were public figures, both in our tight-knit Jewish community and on the campus of Muhlenberg College. Frequently during my elementary years, our Shabbos table on Friday nights included professors, students, Black, white, Latino, Asian, Jews, non-Jews, and people with countless opinions about the news of the day.

By middle school and high school, my mother helped grow Muhlenberg Hillel to be one of the largest and most active campuses in the country. On Friday nights, we would join over two hundred students – diverse Jews, each celebrating our shared faith from a different background, all united for at least a few hours after the sun set on a Friday.

That Black Friday night in 2018, alone with my father, could not have been more different. It was just the two of us, lonely, not knowing how to break the awkward silence. Exhausted, but unable to sleep, I was devastated that I hadn't had the chance to say goodbye. At thirty-five, I had to come to terms with having to spend likely more than half my life without my mother.

That night, I was reminded of the eerily prophetic final line of that op-ed, in which I spoke of our country experiencing a mourning period. At the time, neither my mother nor I knew that within a month, I would be sitting shivah for her, followed by eleven long, introspective months of Jewish mourning traditions.

Recommitting to faith during that period reminded me of the conversations I used to have with my father as a child during our Saturday morning walks to synagogue. He is naturally professorial, so our talks would center around current events, history, and religion. During those Friday night dinners with diverse adults and college students, I was only an observer. But on Saturday morning walks, I got to ask any and all questions.

When eighty-five Jews and passersby were killed in the terrorist bombing of Jewish community center Asociación Mutual Israelita Argentina in

1994 and, the same year, a bomb killed twenty on an Israeli bus on Tel Aviv's Dizengoff Street, my father assured me that horrific terrorist attacks like those had never happened and would never happen to Jews in America. I've always remembered that. I was proud to be a Jew and equally proud to be an American. For many years, my father was right. Ultimately, though, the world changed. The massacre at the Tree of Life Synagogue was just a brutal reminder.

Daniel Korobkin, my rabbi in middle school in Allentown, went on to lead a robust congregation in Toronto. His congregant Robert Libman, just four days after losing his sister in Pittsburgh, delivered a passionate eulogy that was beamed worldwide. He said, "Evil tried to shut out a light, but the light refuses to be dimmed."

Those words spoke to me both then and in the succeeding weeks and months of personal darkness as I grappled with my mother's death. I strived to have a fraction of his courageous optimism.

I believed then, and I certainly believe now, that while the Prophet Isaiah commanded the Jewish people to be a "light unto the nations," there are also individuals outside the Jewish community who go above and beyond to provide *us* rays of comforting light in times of darkness.

"*Kol Yisrael areyim zeh la'zeh*" (All Jews are responsible for one another) was a common expression and value in my childhood home. In times of uncertainty and introspection, there is always significant discussion in the Jewish community about our own leaders rising to the occasion. There is far less focus on those outside the Jewish faith who have gone above and beyond in a way that uplifts our community and inspires their own. My new goal became to find those non-Jewish luminaries who exuded infectious decency and promoted goodwill where and when Jews might have least expected it.

I was still in the research phase of this project when, on the last day of Passover in April 2019, the darkness returned. A gunman opened fire inside the Chabad of Poway in California. At a press conference the following day, the injured Rabbi Yisroel Goldstein stated boldly for the world, "We need to battle darkness with light, no matter how dark the world is."

Regardless of the continent or era, there is a universal pattern to antisemitic acts; they are always responded to with both cowardice and heroism. Many notable works have explored the maddening question of why people didn't help when they could have. We have all read about the cowardly silence of neighbors, coworkers, and fellow citizens during dark times. It is all too easy to point to the bad rather than focus on what is good. I set out to do the latter, and in the days following that heinous attack in Poway, I committed to writing this book in earnest.

When President George W. Bush eulogized his father in December 2018, he used his late father's phrase "a thousand points of light." As my world was still upside down that month, and most nights I could not sleep, I thought a lot about that phrase. I found myself looking for the positive, determined to find at least a handful of those points of light. In the seemingly intensifying antisemitic darkness, I had a gut feeling that leaders committed to deepening the relationship with the Jewish community and the Jewish state were still out there. My hope was that they would inspire me, and if I could actually publish a book, they might inspire my community during these dark times.

In May 2019, I built up the courage to send the first email to get moving on this book, and there was no slowing down. I quickly learned that all of the individuals I reached out to had a story to tell, and I was reminded of something I learned from my mother: the six most powerful words in the English language are "Let me tell you a story."

The eight exceptional non-Jewish leaders featured in this book have gone above and beyond for Israel and for the Jewish people. The group comprises four men and four women – Black, white, and Latino – from different generations and different continents. Some I had known personally for years, a few I had worked with, and others were one degree removed from me.

They are all righteous individuals who have traveled their own unique paths. Never was it the easiest or most lucrative path, but they traveled on because it was the right thing to do. Each of these stories can be read in a single sitting. Although they go well beyond a simple retelling of each individual's résumé, I encourage you to do your own research about their remarkable accomplishments and keep in mind that the stories that follow are merely snapshots of their incredible lives.

The more I spoke with each person, the more I realized that each possessed unique values and attributes that allowed them to serve as lights during times of darkness. When combined, those attributes provide a blueprint for what it means to pursue a righteous path.

The eighteenth-century leader Rabbi Israel ben Eliezer, commonly known as the Baal Shem Tov, compared light to secrets. These individuals provided me with light in a dark time when they shared their secrets with me. I hope they do the same for you.

I will admit that I do not possesses all of their attributes myself, but I hope these stories can inspire those who have the potential to do great things to seek out the righteous path no matter how hidden it may seem during times of darkness. In a world with far too many examples of bad, these pages seek to illuminate the good.

CHAPTER 1
Aston Bright
Flexibly Assertive

"Aston, we're going to need your help. The fires…they're overwhelming!"

That statement might be expected, even routine, for a firefighter. But when Aston Bright received this call, he felt uneasy. It wasn't from the local fire station in Plantation, Florida, where he had volunteered for the past four years. It was from Israel, over six thousand miles away, where he was a member of the Emergency Volunteers Project (EVP).

That Wednesday was a rare night off for Aston. He was exhausted and looking forward to a quiet night at home. Strangely, he had been watching *Fauda,* an Israeli spy series, on Netflix when he was told that he would have to leave in two days for a two-week deployment to Sderot, Israel, to help the local fire department fight fires near Gaza. No longer able to concentrate on the show, he gave up on his quiet night and began packing.

His helmet, tools, and bulky, soot-covered boots took up most of the space in his enormous Plantation Fire Department duffle bag. He had only a small "go bag" for the rest of his clothes, which he filled with T-shirts, underwear, and bunker gear. Suits and ties would not be necessary for this trip.

Much was still unknown – he didn't even know where he'd be sleeping, and he pictured himself set up in a tent somewhere near the Gaza border. With his flight two days away, he had to clear his schedule and touch base with friends and family. In the back of his mind, he couldn't help but wonder if he would be coming back at all.

Aston had been deployed to Israel the previous year, but this trip would be different, for he would be stationed in Sderot instead of Jerusalem. He followed the geopolitics of the Middle East. With his parents emigrating to the United States from Jamaica, he had developed an interest in history and foreign affairs at a young age. In 2005, Israel unilaterally moved nine thousand of its citizens and all military forces outside Gaza's current boundaries. Two years later, Hamas terrorists overthrew the Palestinian National Authority and declared Gaza a military dictatorship. Sderot was located within a mile of the Gaza border. Since early 2018, when it had been announced that the United States planned to move its embassy from Tel Aviv to Jerusalem, the tension across the region had been escalating. What began as protests on the border of Gaza and Israel evolved into attacks by Hamas terrorists using balloons and kites to fly over the border and start devastating fires on Israeli land. Nature preserves and wheat fields were being destroyed, and even the Israeli honeybee industry was devastated. The fires were now out of control, and that's what Aston would be up against in just a few days.

As he thought of people he'd need to call, he tried to prepare answers for the questions he anticipated being asked: *Why do this as a volunteer? Why leave your family for two weeks? Why risk your life fighting fires in Israel?*

A Call to Action

Aston had learned about the EVP in 2016 when the organization was looking for a meeting venue in Broward County, Florida. As someone who always found a way to help others, Aston arranged for them to use the enormous conference room at the Plantation Fire Department headquarters. He liked to show off the station's new facilities and AV equipment, but his interest ran deeper than that. Having studied political science at the University of Florida, he was fascinated with Israel and believed the country to be America's best friend as well as its ally in the Middle East.

Aston joined the dozens of prospective volunteers who had signed up months in advance to listen to the EVP representatives explain how the program worked and why Israel so desperately needed help. It all started in 2006, after the Second Lebanon War. According to Adi Zahavi, the director general of the Emergency Volunteers Project, it became clear that the number of emergency incidents during crisis and wartime was greater than Israel's emergency service personnel could handle, even when working at full capacity.

The already thin Israeli staff was strained, so the EVP was created in 2010 to provide much-needed assistance by training eighteen hundred volunteer first responders from all over the world to work on the front lines alongside the professionals in Israel. Soon after, Israel decided to nationalize and modernize its firefighting force after the devastating Mount Carmel Forest Fire, which forced seventeen thousand people to evacuate and claimed the lives of forty-four. It was the largest fire in Israeli history, burning almost 8,650 acres over four days, but with help from many allied countries, it was extinguished. The cause was unknown.

Israel went from a municipality-based force to a unified national force, but even with these changes, it still has far fewer firefighters than comparable developed countries. During wartime, Israeli firefighters fight more fires in two weeks than most cities and counties do in a year. They also do it severely understaffed: New York City has about eleven thousand firefighters to serve a population of 8.6 million. Israel has a population of over nine million and only two thousand firefighters.

Born with a go-big-or-go-home attitude, Aston jumped at the opportunity to participate in the practical training session in Fort Lauderdale the following day. He signed up for the course, cleared his schedule, and joined the rest of the volunteers at the Fort Lauderdale Fire Rescue Station in the Executive Airport. As a recreational pilot who had earned his single-engine license, he found it a treat to get a behind-the-scenes look at the airport, where the wealthy elite kept their private jets. But the sentiment was short-lived; he was there for a different reason.

The language of firefighting is universal, but the equipment used in Israel is quite different, so Jerusalem firefighters and former members of the Israel Defense Forces Asaf and Arik trained the volunteers in the Israeli way of fighting fire. They also tested everyone's physical limits, everything from running the hose and charging the line to setting up position. After a day of doing rigorous drills, Aston was one of fifteen who earned his certificate.

There is a picture from 9/11 of a firefighter, Mike Kehoe, going up the stairs of the World Trade Center while terrified people run down. It's an image

Aston thinks about frequently. He was twenty-eight when 9/11 rocked the US, and it inspired him to become a firefighter. Like that hero in the stairway, firefighters stepped up and answered the cry for help when America needed it most. But who was doing that for the people of Israel? When the Jewish people needed help during WWII, nobody responded until it was almost too late. For the second time in his life, Aston felt a moral duty to answer that call, so, once he was vetted and his background check approved, he became a certified member of the EVP.

It's not easy putting your professional and personal life on hold and traveling to a foreign country for two weeks with almost no notice. That's why some fire departments don't want their people to get involved with an organization like the EVP – it's too much of a disruption and could leave them short-staffed. But Aston never experienced any of that. When he was deployed to Jerusalem in September 2017, he had the full support of the Plantation Fire Department.

Despite his training, it took Aston a little while to get used to the Israeli methods. Even the trucks were different. The armor-plated, bulletproof fire engines were made by Mercedes and came equipped with Kevlar vests and helmets. The fire engines were smaller so they could maneuver the narrow streets of Jerusalem, and even then, sometimes the trucks had to park five hundred to a thousand feet away from a fire. The handlines on their trucks, the ones the firefighters physically held, were smaller – an inch in diameter compared to the inch and three-quarter American lines – which made for higher water pressure.

The Israeli accountability system was different too. In Plantation, firefighters have placards with their names Velcroed to their helmets. When they arrive on the scene, they place their placards on the truck at a designated station to make it clear where every firefighter is at all times. That's not how they do it in Israel; their system is a little more archaic. They simply have the dispatcher read off the names of everyone on the truck as it leaves the station.

During Aston's first deployment to Jerusalem in 2017, his unit had to disarm a bomb in a tunnel and witnessed a would-be suicide bomber being shot and killed as he tried to run through a checkpoint.

Despite the violence, that's not what stood out for Aston. It was the people he met and the food he ate. He found Jewish people rivaled Jamaicans in their love of food. When they were cleaning up after breakfast, they were already talking about lunch. He quickly learned that hummus was not a garnish, and as a man with a love of good food, he found himself in pursuit of the perfect hummus.

Red Alert

The positive memories from Aston's first deployment shifted to the back of his mind as he watched the latest developments in Gaza unfold on a television in Newark Liberty International Airport during his nine-hour layover in 2018. After a dawn flight from Fort Lauderdale to Newark, he was stuck in the airport with nowhere to go. His anxiety continued to build as he learned more about the situation. There had been $1.4 million of economic loss in Israel, mostly from dozens of acres of fertile farmland being destroyed during the height of the growing season. Nine firefighting teams and four air tankers were working around the clock to battle seven square miles of land ravaged by fire. To make a bad situation worse, summer temperatures in Israel are becoming hotter than ever before.

Seeing CNN International broadcasting from Israel on the airport television screen brought the articles on Aston's phone to life. It was the first time he had seen terrorists using kites and balloons to start fires, but he learned, as he continued to kill time on his phone, that fire balloons were first used in 1849 when the Austrians launched two hundred of them over the city of Venice. They had even been used in the United States; the only American casualties on the mainland during WWII were in Bly, Oregon, when six people died because of Japanese fire balloons.

It didn't help Aston's nerves that the Red Alert app used to provide updates on when rockets are fired into Israel kept dinging, spiking his blood pressure with each notification. For a reprieve, he'd check the group text chain with the EVP volunteers who were also en route. He barely knew the other firefighters, waiting in airports across the country, but he found some comfort in knowing that he wasn't doing this alone.

After several hours spent on his phone or pacing the terminal, he still had no appetite but, needing a distraction, he grabbed a seat at the nearest bar and ordered a drink. Never one to dwell on the negative, he quickly reverted to the outgoing guy his friends knew, striking up a conversation with the familiar face sitting next to him.

"Excuse me," he said. "You look like the guy from *Law & Order*."

"I am the guy from *Law & Order*," said Vincent D'Onofrio. He had a big, bushy beard, but Aston could tell it was him.

It's hard not to like Aston, whose childlike enthusiasm is contagious, so they hit it off immediately. D'Onofrio bought a round of drinks, and they talked for over an hour. As he got up to leave, D'Onofrio said, "Thanks for what you're doing. Good luck over there."

The drinks and conversation calmed his nerves enough for the extensive additional security at the gate to seem tolerable, which is saying something; the boarding process takes twice as long on flights to Israel. Aston didn't even mind the coach seat. He settled his large frame into the tiny seat and tried to sleep, but that proved more difficult than anticipated on this ten-and-a-half-hour flight. Only minutes after takeoff, a mother started walking up and down the aisle trying to calm her crying baby, with zero success. Somewhere over Europe, as the sun started to rise, other rambunctious children began to get antsy. Aston nodded in and out, but the motley crew who had taken over the cabin prevented him from getting any real sleep.

A First Time for Everything

Before he was even a year old, Aston had traveled with his parents to their native Jamaica. At a young age, he developed a hunger to see the world, learn about different cultures, and travel off the beaten path. He had been to thirty-three countries, but he had never been on a flight where he had to have his seatbelt fastened upon entering a country's airspace. Even though they were still seventy-five minutes from Tel Aviv, the captain announced those instructions over the PA. No further explanation was needed. Everyone knew exactly why that rule was put into place.

At that moment, Aston's entire mindset shifted. His senses heightened, and the seriousness of the situation sunk in. His gaze shifted to the tiny window, and he almost expected to see a rocket approach from the ground and blow them out of the sky. For a brief moment, he even doubted his decision. *What in the world have I gotten myself into?*

Naturally, no rocket emerged. The plane landed safely, and as Aston got off the plane, he exited one nightmare scenario and found himself in another: the chaos of Ben-Gurion International Airport. It was Saturday, the Sabbath, which was supposed to be the Jewish day of rest, but hundreds of people were walking in every direction, talking in a dozen languages. Ben-Gurion is a modern airport with distinctive Jerusalem stone, but the extremely long lines at customs dampened Aston's spirits. It had been about thirty hours since he showered or got any real sleep. With bags in hand, all he wanted was to get into the car arranged by the EVP and meet the rest of the American volunteers. They were scheduled to spend the night in Jerusalem before deploying to Sderot the following day.

It felt like a minor victory to make it out of the airport, and he took a deep breath of fresh air to celebrate. He made his way to the end of the terminal only to discover there was no car waiting for him. There was no man holding a sign with his name on it. He powered up his phone and dialed his contact at the EVP as he got his first dose of Israeli summer heat.

"Don't worry about it, brother," the man responded, then directed him to the line for the *sherut* (shared-ride van). A blast of vehicle exhaust hit his nose, and he wilted in the heat. He was in another line and forced to deal with another delay. When he finally got in the shared van, the driver didn't speak English, so Aston showed him the address and sat back to try to enjoy the long ride into Jerusalem.

It felt good to be back in Israel, but he couldn't help but look at the country through a different lens after learning about the escalating conflict over the last two days. Even the security barriers and extensive camera network on the highways stood out more than they had during his previous visit. Almost one million people were living in Jerusalem, and the ancient city was growing by the month. The distinct culture mixed Israeli innovation with priceless history. Yet only five fire stations existed to protect the capital of the Holy Land.

Day 1

The song "Toy," performed by Netta Barzilai, had won the 2018 Eurovision Song Contest for Israel two months before Aston's arrival. He hadn't yet been in the country twenty-four hours, and he must have heard it ten times. It was playing again when he arrived at the Israel Defense Forces Southern Command headquarters Sunday morning for the first briefing.

Aston and the other Americans arrived early and got the chance to meet their Israeli counterparts, who were sleep deprived and beaten down but still warm and welcoming. It was clear that the Americans had arrived just in time. Captain Mikhail was the man in charge, and even though he spoke very little English, he went out of his way to be an accommodating host, referring to the Americans as his "honored guests."

Aston may have been a large Black man from Florida, the son of Jamaican immigrants, but he immediately felt right at home in Israel. The population was as diverse as any other country he had been to, and this group of firefighters were no exception. Some had parents born elsewhere in the Middle East, some had family in Ukraine and Russia, and one firefighter's parents were from Ethiopia.

He had learned on his first trip that no fire department briefing would be complete without food, but they were given a special treat that morning when a group of women arrived at the station with plates of food and native dishes. It was a heartfelt welcome, although it was one meant for the cast of the television show *Chicago Fire*, as that's who the women understood was coming to town. When they finally learned the truth, they were more amused than disappointed; real, well-built American firefighters were a close second.

The Americans were made to feel at home, although the danger of the situation was always in the back of their minds. Every Sderot resident remembered the 2014 fire in a paint factory, which was burned to the ground after being hit by a rocket from the nearby Gaza Strip. The locals had learned how to live with the threat, but Aston and the Americans were new to this.

The military-style morning briefing, complete with PowerPoint presentations, was something else that never happened back in the States. It was during that Sunday morning briefing that Aston was introduced to the Southern District fire chief, Shmulik Friedman. An imposing figure with a shaved head, Friedman had bags under his eyes. He looked like he had been up for days, and he probably had. The tiredness Aston had experienced in his life, he thought, was nothing compared to what this man had endured.

When the meeting started, Friedman's presence alone was enough to capture everyone's attention. He made a passionate speech, describing Israel as a garden that was landscaped by God and cultivated by His children. The terrorist attacks were destroying that garden, and it was up to everyone in that room to help rescue the people, economy, wildlife, and environment. Friedman seemed to get most emotional when he mentioned the practically extinct Negev Desert tortoise. It was the type of speech that Aston had never heard given in a firehouse before. This wasn't just a job for Friedman; it was personal. Suddenly, all the fear and apprehension that had built inside him since getting that Wednesday night call was replaced by a desire to help.

Afterward, the entire group went outside to pose for a photo in front of the firehouse. Above them, Psalm 104:4 was written in Hebrew. When asked for a translation, the Israeli firefighters started arguing about who could render it best, before settling on "Those who extinguish and tame fires are like angels."

The Fire

The Great March of Return was launched on March 30, 2018, when around ten thousand Palestinian protestors set up tent camps along the Gaza border. They demanded the "right of return" to the land from which they believe their ancestors were wrongfully evicted. The protest became violent on both sides. Knowing that the wind blows east from the Mediterranean, protestors used helium to fly incendiary balloons and kites carrying Molotov cocktails over the border. Israeli Defense Forces drones destroyed five hundred kites, but the ones that slipped through created a tremendous amount of damage to a landscape that was dry from the summer sun. The Israeli government struggled not only to extinguish fires, but to reimburse scared and angry farmers.

These were all developments Aston had watched on the news and read about, but the scope of the devastation was difficult to comprehend until he was there. Nothing had prepared him for what he encountered on a Sunday afternoon when he found himself standing at the end of a hose line in a treeless, bone-dry wheat field, fighting a fire started by Hamas about half a mile away from the Gaza border. The hot summer sun bore down on the group from overhead, and the wind blew the smell of devastation in their direction. If any of the volunteers still had any doubts about why their help was needed, they were assured that afternoon.

The Israelis were used to the desert climate, and many of them were fresh out of the military, but this was new for most of the Americans. The playbook they relied on when fighting structure fires back in the States quickly went out the window in this new environment. They were engaged in an hourslong battle of attrition that didn't have an end in sight. That afternoon, Aston was reminded of the classic Mike Tyson quote, "Everyone has a plan until they get punched in the mouth."

When the wind shifted once again, Aston needed to step away for a moment to catch his breath. The heavy gear had sapped his energy, and his eyes burned from the smoke. He could feel the soot in his nostrils and couldn't help but think that the smell of burning wheat wasn't bad compared to the smell of the last structure fire he had fought back in Florida. He had only one experience fighting massive brushfires in Florida, when he had joined the Broward County Strike Team in April 2017 during a rare disaster, the West Mims Wildfire, which most Florida residents will remember.

Fighting a wildfire is a living hell. Given a choice, any firefighter Aston knew would rather run into a burning building. Out in an open field, you often aren't wearing an oxygen tank or mask. You're exposed to the soot and the heat for hours. The elements are harsh, but it's the unpredictability and unlimited fuel that make wildfires so dangerous.

The way to fight any fire is to break one of the four links of the fire tetrahedron: heat, fuel, oxygen, and the chemical chain reaction. When it comes to fighting a wildfire, the strategy is to cut off the fuel source by digging trenches in the direction that the fire is headed. Then you can fight the fire from behind, in the area that's already been burned. Once the fire reaches the trench, it has nowhere to go and no new fuel to consume. The way that firefighters can lose their lives is when they attempt to fight the fire from an area that has yet to be burned. When the wind changes and directs the fire toward where they're standing, they get trapped. That's true in Israel; it's true in Plantation, Florida; and it's true all over the world.

As Aston looked up to the sky, he spotted another kite in the distance before it disappeared below the horizon. He feared that he might be witnessing the start of another disaster. When the wind shifted again, he rushed back to the front of the line. He had to get used to the conditions sooner or later. It wouldn't be like this only today. It would be like this every day.

"To Redeem the Soul"

A cultural nuance that was lost on Aston – and is probably lost on most Americans – is the strict observance of the Sabbath by many in Israel. Naturally, when a building catches fire, all bets are usually off. But on Aston's second Saturday in Israel, a local synagogue caught fire, and the firefighters didn't learn about it for twenty minutes because nobody wanted to use a phone to call for help. He might not have understood, but he admired the level of devotion.

That day, after a week of battling wildfires out in the hot, summer sun, both the Israelis and the Americans had been looking forward to some relaxing time off. But the day of rest was cut short when the call eventually came in that afternoon. The Americans felt a rush. This was what they were used to – racing to put on their gear, hopping on the truck, and flying out of the station on their way to the structure fire. This was their time to teach their Israeli hosts how things were done back in their country.

Although the situation seemed familiar, the cultural differences were still noticeable. As the bright red Mercedes engine ripped through the tight Israeli streets, Aston realized that he still hadn't grown used to the offbeat sound of the siren. Even stranger, the driver beside him asked that *he* navigate, barking at him to use Google Maps. He did not know whether to feel a sense of pride or desperation. Earlier in the week, she had caught him walking out of the shower only in a towel, but, their awkward encounter now forgotten, they communicated flawlessly as Aston called out the directions of street names that he had no idea how to pronounce. As she turned the large wheel and peeled around the corners, all she would say was "*Sababa*" (Cool).

Thick black smoke billowed out of the synagogue as the engine arrived on the scene. It was a one-story stone building that was about twenty-five hundred square feet. Back in Florida, there would have been thirty or so people there already – police officers, paramedics, and firefighters organizing the scene and battling the blaze. But Israel just didn't have the manpower, so they were only the second vehicle to arrive. Without anyone there to control the crowd, congregants – from preteens to elderly men – were running in and out of the burning building trying to save prayer books and Bibles. Some were even trying to carry out the pews and furniture. They took the most care trying to remove the Torah scrolls, even though it meant putting their own lives at risk.

Aston had never seen anything like it, and it caused him to pause for a moment before he got out of the truck to yell at the congregants to keep their distance. Even with an imposing American yelling at them, the older men were determined to save the sacred text. They turned the tables and started yelling back at Aston. The chaos was amplified by the chatter coming over the radio, all in Hebrew. Not only did he not speak the language, but there seemed to be no order to what was happening, and time was precious.

The fire had been burning for over twenty minutes, and fires can double in size every sixty seconds. Before they could start dousing the building with water, they needed to flake the hose, a task Aston had performed a thousand times before. Instinct kicked in, and he began laying out the massive hose so that it wouldn't whip around and become a weapon when the pressurized water started blasting though. They were just about ready to hook up the five-hundred-gallon tanker to the hydrant on the right side of the building when more firefighters arrived on the scene.

Unlike the United States, most of the buildings in Israel are made of stone, which means the structure won't catch fire, just the contents inside. That doesn't make it any less dangerous. Even steel will melt above 1,000 degrees. When all of the items inside start burning, it turns into what Aston has dubbed "methyl-ethyl bad shit." A couple puffs of that and you're unconscious, which is why it's often smoke that kills people, not fire.

Despite the stone structure, they couldn't barge in and start spraying water around the room without ventilating it first. When fighting structure fires in Israel, steam becomes a fatal threat. Picture dumping water into a brick pizza oven. The canary in the coal mine is when you start to feel your ears burn through the Nomex hoods the firefighters wear under their helmets. That's the sign that it's time to get out.

Once the building was ventilated, all seven firefighters moved in unison and worked together. No longer were cultural or language differences a barrier; Aston trusted every single firefighter in that building, and they trusted him. It felt like they had been working together for years. Everything was, indeed, *sababa*.

Within the hour, the fire had been extinguished, and they were able to save much of the contents of the synagogue. The firefighters exited to applause from the people who gathered outside. The same men who had scrambled to rescue the books and furniture were already on their way back inside for evening prayers to conclude the Sabbath. Aston didn't have the energy to stop them and knew that they wouldn't listen to him if he tried, so he let them go. As they reached the truck and started loading the gear, the Israeli firefighters were already talking about dinner that night.

You Can't Go Home Again

Shakshuka is a colorful Mediterranean dish with eggs poached in a spicy tomato sauce. That was just one of the main dishes served during the going-away dinner at the firehouse, the night before the Americans returned home. Over the previous two weeks, *shakshuka* had become Aston's favorite food, though he couldn't pronounce it correctly – something the Israeli firefighters teased him mercilessly about for the entire stay after he corrected their pronunciation of his name. The closest they came was "Austin" or "Austen"; even when he tried to have them translate it directly into Hebrew, they still couldn't do it, and it became a running joke that never seemed to get old. Now that the shoe was on the other foot, it felt like poetic justice for the Israeli hosts.

They didn't just have dinner that night; they had a feast and stayed up late, telling jokes and reliving stories from the previous two weeks. Despite all they encountered, the spirits of Captain Mikhail and the Israeli firefighters never dampened.

One of Aston's most memorable moments in Israel occurred when they were at an IDF safehouse in Nahal Oz along the Gaza border. The commander in charge of the Southern Division took him and a few of the volunteers through the kibbutz and up into the observation tower to look out over Gaza. As they climbed the ladder, he warned, "If snipers start shooting at us, I want you guys to climb down and meet me at the base of the building." If what he said wasn't alarming enough, the casual way he said it was even more unsettling. The tower was twenty feet away from the fence that lined the demilitarized zone between Israel and Gaza, and Aston wasn't taking any chances. At the top, he made sure to turn his hat around so that its American flag would not be visible to anyone watching him from a distance.

All the Israeli people Aston met were friendly, even the military personnel. While out in the field one afternoon, the firefighters came across an Israeli tank that had been patrolling the border only hours earlier. The soldiers allowed them to sit inside the tank, and everyone took pictures and posted them to social media. Within minutes, Aston was getting texts from people back home wondering what he had gotten himself into.

Aston enjoyed his final meal with his Israeli hosts, but it felt bittersweet. He knew that for the communities living in the Gaza envelope, the fight was far from over. His group of American volunteers was leaving the following day, but a new group would take their place and pick up right where they left off. *Did they make a difference? How much progress had they made? When will all this end and the region see peace?* The questions played on a loop in his head. He couldn't imagine going to work every single day under these conditions, but this battle had become a way of life for the Israeli firefighters, for whom he had developed a profound respect after watching the way they worked tirelessly to save their people and their homeland.

"Return to the United States and tell everyone what you saw" is what Shmulik Friedman told Aston and the others to do upon returning home. And that's precisely what he did.

Today, Aston doesn't miss an opportunity to speak publicly about the Jewish people and the cause he risked his life to support. In the months that followed his time in Sderot, Aston addressed audiences in New York, Maryland, Georgia, and across his beloved Florida. To his surprise, it is a cause that many Americans are unaware of, judging by the expressions on the faces in the crowd when he starts rattling off statistics.

He explains in his talks how between May and August 2018, over a thousand fires were started in southern Israel, some by terrorists using rudimentary weapons. The last day Aston was in Israel, there were twenty-six fires. The previous *year* in Plantation, there were only thirty-six.

Aston always had a soft spot for Israel and considered the nation and its citizens friends. But through two life-changing deployments in Israel and talking to diverse Jewish American audiences, he realized that he was wrong. They weren't just his friends. Israel and the Jewish people were family.

CHAPTER 2

Markus Stötzel
Zealously Advocating

It all started with a favor.

In 1998, Markus Stötzel was thirty-two years old and, after six long years of school, he was right where he wanted to be. He had just passed the second *Staatsexamen* (state exam), which is the German equivalent of the bar exam. Having settled down in Marburg, he was excited to begin his career working as a lawyer for a fast-growing real estate company in nearby Frankfurt, which had become the financial capital of postwar Germany. His future was all mapped out when he was approached by a close friend. "There's an older woman in the neighborhood who's been looking for help."

"With a real estate question?" Markus assumed.

"In a way. She put in an application immediately after reunification to get her childhood property in West Berlin back and is at a dead end. She went to another firm in Marburg, but it was too complicated a legal matter for them."

"But I'm not an expert in that field either."

"I know, but her appeal is due, and she's running out of time. She's been asking me what she can do, but I don't know how to help her. Would you at least sit down with her?"

It was far out of his area of expertise, but, always up for a challenge, Markus called up Dorothea and arranged for her to come to his office on a Friday afternoon. He wasn't looking to take on any pro bono work and, knowing nothing about ever-changing property restitution laws, he doubted he would be able to help her at all. Perhaps he could make a few calls.

Markus expected his meeting with Dorothea to last an hour. Two hours later, he was still captivated by her stories of a childhood in high society interrupted by the rise of National Socialism. The usually charming, talkative Markus remained silent that afternoon and listened intently.

Dorothea's grandfather was a well-known professor before he died in 1914, and the family inherited his mansion on the Voßstraße (Voss Strasse), the most famous boulevard in Berlin. The family hosted lavish dinner parties for the city's elite during the Roaring Twenties, but life quickly changed with the rise of the Third Reich. The lifestyle they had grown accustomed to came to an end shortly after 1933 when the Nazis forced the family to abandon their home. Dorothea was in her early teens, and she vividly remembers her father having his arm broken by a Schutzstaffel (SS) officer when he tried to fight back. There was nothing they could do. The land was seized to begin construction of the grand Reich Chancellery. The family remained in Berlin during the war but spent the final years hiding in a cottage on the outskirts of the city until liberation in May 1945. The conditions were dire, and they faced the constant threat of being deported to death camps, but a few brave souls provided them with food and the essentials they needed to survive.

That night, Markus couldn't get Dorothea's story out of his mind. She remembered everything with vivid detail and told her story with such passion. She had strong character and a warm heart. He could tell right away that she was not out for revenge; she simply wanted justice for her family, particularly for her father, who died a broken man in 1960, after years of torture and abuse at the hands of the Nazis. That's why Markus agreed to help her.

Dorothea's story was unique. In 1990, the German Jewish population was roughly thirty thousand – down from thirty-seven thousand in 1950 – but was growing significantly. It had more than doubled by 2002 with reunification and the emigration of Jews from the former Soviet Union but was still a tiny fraction of what it had been before the war. Few German Jews decided to remain in Germany after the war. Those who stayed experienced psychological persecution, having to relive traumatic memories.

Even though Markus knew he wouldn't see a dime, he sat down to look into her claim that weekend. While he was working, he realized that Dorothea was the first Jew he had ever met.

Mitläufer

Born in Siegen, West Germany, in 1966, Markus was raised by his mother, a schoolteacher, and his industrial electrician father. But it was his elderly grandfather on his mother's side who made the biggest impression; not only had he lived through both World Wars and survived a POW camp, he had been a member of the National Socialist Party. Put simply, he had been a Nazi in a past life.

The Cold War was escalating when Markus entered high school in 1980. The United States and sixteen other countries were boycotting the Moscow Olympics. Markus's interest in politics and world events grew along with the turmoil and intrigue of the times. Soon, that interest extended to history – German history, in particular. The education his generation received about the atrocities of the Holocaust was arguably more extensive than it was in the United States at the time, but the East and West German school systems each took a different approach. While the aim of the West German system was to strengthen its new democratic order, schools in the East focused on socialism. Debates raged about how to address the time period, which became known as the *Historikerstreit* (historians' dispute) in West Germany in the eighties. When the Berlin Wall came down, laws against Holocaust denial were created, and a more unified school system addressing Holocaust education began to emerge.

When Markus was in school, it was common for kids to have relatives who had fought in the war and were even members of the Nazi Party, so his situation was not unusual. But Markus wasn't interested in war stories, and his grandfather wasn't forthcoming with details. Markus was more interested in politics, particularly philosophical arguments about the role of government and its relationship with minority citizens. He felt there was no better source of information than his grandfather, so he frequently made the thirty-minute trip to where he lived to spend hours talking with him. The very real specter of war with the Soviet Union loomed, but often the conversation would drift back to the past, to WWII and its aftermath.

Mitläufer (follower) was a term Markus had heard frequently growing up, but he didn't know what it meant until his grandfather explained that it was used to describe people like himself: a soldier, citizen, or Nazi Party member who went along with the regime. As a teenager, the budding lawyer in Markus learned how to persuade his reticent grandfather to open up about serving in

North Africa under General Rommel during his infamous desert campaigns and then being sent to a British POW camp.

When the war was over, the Allies created a structure to classify Germans into five groups:

1. Major offenders.
2. Offenders.
3. Lesser offenders.
4. Followers.
5. Exonerated persons.

His grandfather fell into the fourth category, a follower, and the most difficult for jurists in the wake of the war (and even modern-day historians) to define. It was these discussions with his grandfather that planted the seed in Markus for a possible career in law, but first, he studied political science and economics at the University of Siegen. It was when East and West Germany officially reunified to become the Federal Republic of Germany on October 3, 1990, that he decided on a career in law, and once he set his mind to something, he did not waver.

East Germany dissolved overnight, and the new country entered uncharted territory. The differences between East and West Germany went far beyond politics; freedom of movement was taken for granted in the democracy of West Germany, but in East Germany a police state had emerged under socialist control. The just under sixteen million citizens who had been living in an authoritarian country had little in common with those from the West. Daily life was drastically different, too: food, cultural programs, school curriculum, and even vacation destinations were alien to East Germans, and the stark contrast extended to architecture and overall atmosphere. Whereas the buildings in the former East Germany were sterile and functional, Markus felt the cityscape in the West was vibrant and alive.

In a modern world that was becoming increasingly technology driven, marrying the legal codes of the two countries would prove chaotic. Just thinking of the countless real estate cases that would arise in the years ahead got Markus excited about his future career prospects. Meanwhile, he honed his talent. While working as a part-time tax advisor after graduating with a law degree from Phillips Marburg University, he discovered that he had a knack for finding practical solutions to problems by observing data – a skill that would aid him in ways that he could never have predicted.

From the Textbook to the Real World

From a legal perspective, Dorothea did everything correctly when she submitted a formal application after reunification in 1990, but her parents had drafted their will as if the Iron Curtain would never fall. Back in the 1960s, Dorothea had received a payment from her parents that was offset against her share of their future estate, so she no longer qualified as an heir, and her claim was dismissed. The property was considered "heirless," and under the law was awarded to the Claims Conference, an organization which, ironically, seeks justice for Jewish Holocaust victims and has been negotiating with the German government since shortly after WWII.

After spending a string of late nights delving deep into German civil and inheritance law, Markus came up with an unorthodox plan to apply for a new inheritance document for Dorothea. He argued that since East Germany was no longer a country, the original forms were null and void. Had Dorothea's parents known that Germany would be reunited and that it was possible to get back looted property, they would not have excluded her as an heir. It was a skillful legal argument that Markus remains proud of to this day.

This aspect of the law wasn't always the first priority of the new, reunified German government. The country was still trying to consolidate the East and West telephone systems, so trying to get a simple call back from the archives or the courthouse was no easy task. With the internet still in a nascent stage, it was imperative that Markus show up in person and become a squeaky wheel or else risk being overlooked. So, with the new application under review, Markus traveled with Dorothea to Berlin, which had become the new German capital.

Having grown up on the other side of the Wall, Markus assumed that there would always be two German states. Even eight years after reunification, the idea of one united Germany was a difficult concept to comprehend. When looking around the city, he realized that he was not in the Berlin he had read about in textbooks. In June 1991, the Bundestag (parliament) voted to move the West German capital of Bonn to Berlin, so the city was in the middle of a lot of change. The massive move would not be until 1999, and the cultural shift was equally jarring, but the east side of the city had not entirely erased its cold and sterile past.

The streets of Berlin were a new sight for Markus, but they brought back bittersweet childhood memories for Dorothea. After weeks spent listening to her talk about her family and devouring the records, Markus started to feel like the property he was fighting so hard for was a part of his own past. When he laid eyes on it for the first time, he realized how different the reality was. The surroundings were distinctly East German: concrete and seemingly permanently stained with air pollution. No new buildings were nearby, a stark reminder of the authoritarianism that marked East Germany – even now, eight years after reunification. He was surprised by the condition of the building and wondered why she had gone to so much trouble. His reaction wasn't lost on Dorothea, who joked that if she regained ownership of the property, she would allow him and his family to use it as a vacation home.

The German legal system reminded Markus of the subtitled Wild West movies he had watched as a boy to help him learn English. New case law was being made by the month, and the textbooks he had studied less than a decade previously were quickly becoming irrelevant. There was often no established precedent, making it difficult to navigate, so Markus chose to accompany Dorothea on her many trips to the courthouse over the next months. Sometimes they drove. Sometimes they took the train. He slowly started to feel he was becoming a part of the family, although he made sure to keep a professional distance. In the end, their persistence paid off: Dorothea was granted rights to the property, a decision that took retroactive effect and could not be appealed. The victory was much more personal than professional for Markus, for he worked entirely pro bono.

On the drive back home to Marburg, Dorothea said, "My family had an art collection on the walls of my childhood home. Let's look into getting that back, too!"

The Monuments Men

George Clooney, Matt Damon, Bill Murray, John Goodman, Cate Blanchet, and an all-star supporting cast shed a very bright spotlight on the unlikely American platoon tasked with recovering artwork stolen by the Nazis during WWII in the 2014 film *The Monuments Men.*

In the early years of the Third Reich, the Nazis attempted to fund their war machine through looted art, statues, silver, and porcelain collections, all of which could be resold for a pretty penny in the 1930s. They made sure to carefully document every sale – especially those with Jewish owners. They kept meticulous records so they wouldn't be accused of forcing Jews to sell below market rates while under duress, a detail that plagued the restitution process for decades to come when these forced sales would become the subject of court cases. When the Nuremberg Race Laws were enacted in 1935, the Nazis put even more pressure on Jewish owners to sell. These efforts climaxed with Kristallnacht on November 9–10, 1938, when the Nazis plundered Jewish-owned businesses, homes, community organizations, and synagogues. Around a hundred Jews were killed, and thirty thousand were sent to concentration camps. Dachau had been operating for the previous five years, and Sachsenhausen and Buchenwald had recently been built, in 1936 and '37, respectively. The city of Siegen was not exempt from the violence; a synagogue was torched, and eleven Jewish men were sent to camps.

The Nazis were so successful in their plunder that they created units called *Kunstschutz* to acquire valuables and works of art until the end of the war. Hitler, an unsuccessful artist, still considered himself an expert critic and had plans to create a separate museum called the Führermuseum for the stolen artwork near his birthplace in Linz, Austria. He hoped to revitalize the city and turn it into the cultural capital of the Third Reich, a passion project for Hitler. He had a scale model on display by January 1945, and plans were underway for construction to be completed in 1950.

In April 1945, the US Army's 8th Infantry Division made its way to Siegen, and the real-life Monuments Men discovered an extensive mine network containing a massive collection of stolen, priceless works of art by Cézanne, Rembrandt, Renoir, Rubens, and Van Gogh. Cases containing artifacts taken from museums in Bonn, Cologne, Wuppertal, Essen, and Munster were discovered along with cases containing treasures from cathedrals throughout Europe. The finds included the original manuscript of Beethoven's Sixth Symphony and a bust of Charlemagne. Among the thousands of pieces were the untold stories of Jewish owners surrendering precious family heirlooms at gunpoint.

Even after the unconditional surrender of Nazi Germany on May 8, 1945, the war-ravaged conditions of European cities, lack of reliable communication, and the sheer size of the recovered collection in the mines below Markus's hometown and a vast network of other storage depots made the process of provenance research all but impossible. The haul from the Siegen mine was massive, but it was only the start. Tens of thousands of pieces of priceless art were discovered by the Monuments Men in the months and years to come, and even more were never touched by Allied forces.

The Law Is Not Black or White

During their trips back and forth to Berlin, Dorothea told Markus stories about her father and shared family photos. When describing her home before they were forced out, she vividly remembered a marble bust of her father as a young man. She went into tremendous detail about the piece, and Markus used that detail to begin his search. Scouring through records, he miraculously traced it to the Museum der bildenden Künste (Museum of Fine Arts) in Leipzig, the second largest city in the former East Germany, located in the state of Saxony.

Markus brought Dorothea with him to the museum, and they were prepared for a fight, but were pleasantly surprised when they were welcomed with open arms and didn't have to plead their case or try to haggle. The bust was already packaged and ready for immediate transport. Dorothea leaned toward Markus and told him, "We are taking my father home."

Those words meant a lot to Markus, and he found his interest divided at work. He had spent years studying for a career in real estate law, and he enjoyed it, but it was hardly his passion. It didn't make him as energized and excited as helping Dorothea. He couldn't tell right away if that was a good thing; he had taken more legal ethics courses than he cared to remember, and he knew that a lawyer wasn't supposed to be emotionally invested in a client's case. He knew he had to remain objective, but this type of work was different. It required him to be a zealous advocate for his client, and staying neutral when listening to Dorothea relive painful memories from her past was difficult. There wasn't a course or a textbook that could have prepared him for that.

Even with a young family at home in Marburg, Markus spent many nights and weekends working for Dorothea pro bono, and it soon paid off when he found another needle in the haystack. *Afternoon in the Tuileries Gardens* (1867), painted by the famous nineteenth-century German realist Adolph von Menzel, used to hang on Dorothea's Berlin living room and was now in a Dresden museum. Markus made an appointment, and he and Dorothea visited the city in Saxony, which had been extensively bombed by the Allies during the war.

Unlike in Leipzig, there was hostility in the room. No pleasantries were exchanged with the staff. As Markus and Dorothea were escorted into a conference room, Markus immediately realized that his previous experience reclaiming the bust was the exception and not the rule. Nine men were already seated at the table, all born either during the Third Reich or at the height of East Germany. They didn't show any emotion, and their body language was impossible to read. The room was ice cold. "We're sorry you traveled all the way here," said the man at the head of the table, who didn't bother to stand or introduce himself. "But we do not believe that conditions in 1934 and 1935 were that bad, and we know that this painting was sold through a fair process. It will absolutely not leave our museum."

Markus wasn't speaking to museum leadership. He was speaking to an official from the Saxony state government. And they were asking the question that would be at the heart of every restitution case for decades to come: "Was this sale made under duress?" A paper trail isn't beneficial to the victim when the authorities can point to a document bearing a family member's signature. Under other circumstances, it would be difficult to argue that a theft occurred, but when people show up at your house with weapons – often in the middle of the night – and force you to sign a bill of sale and hand over valued possessions, that's not a normal circumstance. However, that's what occurred time and again during the 1930s.

Markus froze and was at a loss for words, but Dorothea filled the void. She spoke in a tone Markus didn't recognize. "Would you like to see the yellow star that I keep to this day? I was forced to wear it on my clothes when the conditions, as you say, were not that bad."

Despite Dorothea's strength, they walked away without the piece that day. It was a wake-up call for Markus, as he realized that pursuing justice wasn't going to be straightforward or linear. As satisfying as his work with Dorothea was, it also involved a unique set of tough-to-stomach challenges that would test his skills. Older clients like Dorothea were emotional and impatient, with good reason, and they put their trust in Markus to retrieve a piece of their heritage and recover something of their past.

The Law on the Settlement of Open Property Issues, which was signed in 1990, provided basis for claimants to reclaim looted or unlawfully taken assets that were located in former East German territory. The new system, albeit a political milestone, was anything but cut and dried. It was difficult to navigate these complex, confusing new legal waters. And Markus and Dorothea weren't alone in being in confusing new territory, as almost every aspect of life was impacted for the people forced to transition to new social, economic, administrative, and legal systems. Since Dorothea's painting was part of the state of Saxony's art collections, she had a legitimate claim, but the state administration vigorously challenged her right and refused its return.

Markus and Dorothea received the support of the Claims Conference, and German media outlets put additional pressure on the museum officials. The optics of withholding property from a Nazi victim's family weren't good, yet the fight dragged on until 2005, when eventually the cultural minister gave in to avoid a growing scandal.

Word quickly spread about a well-spoken, charismatic, bilingual young lawyer who had a knack for retrieving artwork that had been stolen by the Nazis. When calls started coming in, Markus faced a choice: continue down the career path he had so carefully mapped out or take an entirely different route. State authorities had set the bar very high to prove that Nazi oppression had directly contributed to the sale of artwork in the 1930s, but Markus realized that he could help form certain aspects of the new law.

Contrary to how it felt during those first weeks and months with Dorothea, Markus learned that he wasn't alone in this fight. On December 3, 1998, the same year he passed the bar, the Clinton administration hosted leaders from forty-four countries to establish guidelines for Holocaust-era assets to be returned to their prewar owners or else be auctioned for the benefit of Holocaust survivors. The Washington Conference Principles on Nazi-Confiscated Art was an effort that forced museums to reexamine their collections, and an international voluntary framework for restitution slowly developed.

An Impressive Career

Across Germany, Markus went on to become a known fixture in museum boardrooms and among German municipal solicitors and state attorneys. The German press enjoyed seeking quotes from the articulate, persistent advocate with a big mustache. More than once, his efforts have been portrayed as David going up against Goliath.

It was another David-versus-Goliath fight that brought Markus to the United States in the fall of 2015. It was the seventieth anniversary of the end of WWII. The Federal Republic of Germany had paid close to $70 billion to Nazi victims between 1953 and 1995. Yet as Holocaust survivors were dying and their heirs were growing old, German cities, states, and private institutions, arguably, were not living up to the Washington Principles of 1998.

One of the more prominent people advocating that claim was Dr. Michael Hulton, the nephew and heir to Alfred Flechtheim, the most influential art dealer during the avant-garde period just before the Nazis came to power in 1933. Flechtheim was targeted and forced to flee Germany penniless. Although Hulton had been able to recover some of the works in his uncle's collection, including works by Pablo Picasso, he knew many more still hung on walls in Germany. It all came down to the same question that Markus had to prove for Dorothea seventeen years earlier: *Were these sales made under duress?*

Markus had previously teamed up with an Orthodox Jewish lawyer from New York City, Mel Urbach. An equally brilliant legal mind, he realized that the seventieth anniversary provided an opportunity to appeal to what Americans call "the court of public opinion." Markus, Urbach, and Hulton spent a week educating journalists and Jewish community audiences. After a successful day in Washington, DC, they convinced twenty-nine congressmen to sign a bipartisan open letter demanding that the governor of Bavaria, the largest German state and the birthplace of the Nazi Party, answer difficult questions about artwork hanging on the walls of state buildings.

Now, Markus gets compensated if he recovers property for his clients. It was not the lucrative real estate law career he prepared or trained for, but it turned into a lifelong pursuit that has been both an adventure and a passion. George Clooney may have brought the issue to the public attention with *Monuments Men*, but it was Markus, combing through government archives, listening patiently to emotional testimony, and trekking to courthouses only to get critical looks from fellow Germans, who has actually brought justice.

And to think that his career might never have materialized had he not offered to do a favor for a friend.

CHAPTER 3
Olga Meshoe Washington
Meticulously Diligent

It was August 3, 2014, and over twelve thousand diverse South Africans gathered in Johannesburg for a solidarity rally for Israel. They were united in their goal to bring comfort to the local Jewish community. Olga Meshoe Washington was slotted to speak in between two giants – the Israeli ambassador and the chief rabbi of South Africa – but only forty-five minutes before she was supposed to step to the podium, she was nowhere to be found. She wasn't backstage; she was in the parking lot, sitting alone in her car, going over her speech with a fine-tooth comb. This would be the largest crowd she had ever spoken in front of, and she had a chance to make an impact, but her nerves were shot, and she started to second-guess the commitment entirely.

An attorney and active leader for young congregants in church, Olga had only recently been introduced to pro-Israel activism and community by her legendary father, Reverend Kenneth Meshoe of the African Christian Democratic Party. He had helped organize the peace rally, which would be the first of its kind in the history of South Africa, but when he learned that he would not be able to attend, he suggested that Olga take his place. She was hesitant at first and felt entirely unqualified, but he assured her, "You'll do great." That settled it.

The more Olga thought about it, the more she wanted to speak, and the more committed she became to the organizational efforts. First, they had to ensure a significant Black cross-denominational Christian presence at the rally, so they stirred up excitement in the churches and got people to register and commit to attending. They collected the cell phone numbers of all the participants and worked diligently to ensure that no churchgoers backed out. They also had to arrange buses to transport people across the sprawling metro of Johannesburg. As the event drew near, the leaders received threats, and the organizers prepared for disruption and possible violence. Participants were instructed to remain non-violent. With safety measures in place, they pressed on and didn't cave to the threats on the internet.

Like a good attorney, Olga spent two weeks diligently researching what was going on politically. But the enormity of the rally, and her new role in it, created a tremendous amount of stress, and by the day of the event, she was a nervous wreck.

South Africans are political by nature, so a crowd of twelve thousand people at an event like this was not abnormal. What was surprising was the very visible support for Israel from such a diverse assembly of South Africans. That had never happened before, and it only added to the pressure Olga felt as she left her car and made her way to the stage. She had a real opportunity to do something great by motivating and educating the crowd, as well as those who would later watch on television. That opportunity came with responsibility. If she were to mess up or get her data wrong when speaking to a crowd of twelve, it would be unfortunate. But if she messed up in front of twelve thousand, she would have squandered an opportunity to inspire real change. That's why in church that morning, she tuned out her father while he preached and silently went over her speech in the pew. She hoped sequestering herself in her car would ready her, but no amount of studying could have prepared her for stepping onto that stage and gazing out at the sea of thousands of Israeli flags. It was by far the most nerve-racking moment of her life.

No matter what the venue, Olga always set out to be engaging and to grab the audience's attention. So, to do that and to ease her own nerves, she did something that she had never done before, but had seen Ellen DeGeneres do at the recent Academy Awards: she took a selfie. She moved to the front of the stage, turned her back to the enormous, diverse crowd, and raised her cell phone to snap the picture. That immediately calmed her, and when she spoke, the crowd hung on her every word.

Educated about an Alternate History

In 1956, Israeli foreign minister Golda Meir laid out her vision for engaging new countries across Africa emerging from colonial rule. It was a controversial move, since many of those countries had little to offer Israel, but she did so because she believed that Jews shared with the people of Africa a history of discrimination and oppression.

In 1948, the National Party came to power in South Africa, thus beginning what would become the forty-six years of institutionalized racial segregation known as apartheid. One hundred fifty codified laws affected every hour of every day for the majority Black population. For generations, South African Jews worked and lived alongside their Black neighbors. In his autobiography *Long Walk to Freedom,* Nelson Mandela said, "in my experience, I have found Jews to be more broad-minded than most whites on issues of race and politics, perhaps because they themselves have historically been victims of prejudice."

When apartheid came to an end in 1994, Mandela – commonly known as "Madiba," a name of reverence and affection – was elected president. He had left prison just four years earlier. While he continued to speak highly of the Jewish community of South Africa, he spoke out strongly against the Israeli government for their support of the apartheid government – the government that he fought so hard to remove from power – although Israel did curtail that support in the late 1980s. During his five-year stint as president, Mandela, the African National Congress (ANC), and other prominent black South African political leaders such as Nobel Prize winner Reverend Desmond Tutu aligned themselves with anti-Israel, nondemocratic regimes like Castro's Cuba, Gaddafi's Libya, and theocratic leaders in Iran. They sided with the Palestinians in their conflict with Israel, and some went so far as to declare Israel a terrorist state.

In 1999, Mandela's complicated relationship with Israel took another turn when he made a historic visit to the Holy Land. The trip was unprecedented, but it was fraught from the start, as Mandela arrived just after visiting Israel's enemies Syria and Iran. He pushed for a two-state solution, though he never questioned Israel's right to exist.

Mandela's views were not uncommon among South African leaders. There was indeed a period when Israel was not a friend of the South African liberation movement, a fact that was exploited by antisemitic leaders who put their passion and energy into promoting one side of the argument. That manipulated message about the narrative of the Middle East made its way into the South African school system. In the meantime, the ANC had become bold in its love affair with Hamas, who were given a red-carpet welcome when invited to the ANC national conference.

This was the post-apartheid South Africa where Olga came of age, but it did not resemble the Zionist home in which she was raised. In addition to being a parliamentarian and a faith leader, her father was an active advocate for Israel and the Jewish people. He traveled the world and received awards, but Olga wasn't fully aware of the need to advocate for Israel when she was younger. She read about injustice and heard stories of antisemitism, but like many, she didn't stop to make it her problem. She was instead focused on her own path to becoming a doctor, transitioning into law when high school science got in the way. Her youth leadership in the church gave her confidence in public speaking and community organizing, so she quickly moved up the legal ladder. For eight and a half years, she worked in the nicest neighborhood in Johannesburg as a commercial attorney involved in capital markets and became a partner at her firm before turning thirty.

Meanwhile, South Africa's attitude toward Israel had not evolved much since Mandela's time as president. Outside the Muslim world, South Africa had some of the most virulent anti-Israel activists and rampant antisemitic public discourse. Many had been drawn in by the BDS movement, which had since co-opted the apartheid narrative to present Israel as an apartheid state worse than South Africa. Apartheid was still very raw for many South Africans, and most were good-intentioned people who didn't want to see another group of people experience that same kind of suffering, so they latched onto that narrative. It was an easy thing to do, for it was the path of least resistance, if not fashionable, to speak out against Israel on campus and in the professional world.

Olga's father recognized the apartheid comparison as an absolute lie that made a mockery of the struggles his family and the families of all Black South Africans were forced to endure. When he was growing up, white people and Black people were segregated by law. Black people received inferior education and couldn't be in the legislature or even vote. That doesn't resemble Israel, the only multi-party democratic state across the Middle East and North Africa, where there is no segregation by skin color or religion. Arabs and Jews can live, work, and learn together without any legal restrictions.

The reverend knew that people couldn't take their country's history and repackage it just because they wanted to see the demise of another country. He felt that if there was going to be a retort to that claim, it had to come from those who endured unspeakable suffering during apartheid – the Black South African community. That's why he created an organization called DEISI (Defend, Embrace, Invest, Support Israel) in 2013 to deliberately oppose the BDS movement, which had spread widely across Europe and North America and was metastasizing in South Africa. The organization set out to dispel the myth that BDS supporters promulgated at every opportunity that Israel was an apartheid state. They strived to educate, create awareness, and forge new relationships while serving as ambassadors of truth.

It was July 2014 when Olga found herself stepping into the arena and following in her father's footsteps when standing in for him during the day-long conference with South African Jewish leaders. That was her introduction to the community and vice versa. She had traveled to Israel with the church but had never had any meaningful conversations with Jews or understood the human element of the persecution and security concerns that were developing due to the BDS movement. That was quickly about to change.

Return to the Holy Land

After taking the onstage selfie, Olga was able to settle down. She spoke with passion and energy, declaring loud and clear that Israel had friends in South Africa who would defend her right to exist as a sovereign state. She left the audience with two requests: first, to not be bitter about or afraid of those who hate and make unfounded accusations against Israel but to simply brush it off; second, to stand with others who face trials and challenges.

Those in the BDS and anti-Israel movements were shocked to see such passionate support for Israel, but the reality was that people on the ground in South Africa loved Israel, even if they didn't completely understand the politics of the day. Much of that had to do with citizens of both countries being deeply involved in their respective faith communities.

When the dust settled after the event, Israel wasn't the only one who received support. The speech helped make Olga into a minor celebrity in the South African Jewish community. She realized how powerful her voice had become, which further elevated the momentum DEISI had gained over the previous year. She was promoted to chief executive officer of DEISI and made the difficult decision to leave her full-time job at the law firm. She had discovered her true passion, so she parted with the firm and dedicated herself to the new cause.

Her first obligation was to arrange for a group of young South African leaders to travel to Israel for ten days in November 2014. Preparations for the trip had begun before the rally, but Olga dedicated all her time and focus to interviewing prospective students and young leaders now that her speech had been delivered. Both the church and the most influential people in the community helped publicize what was an opportunity of a lifetime, and individuals from every corner of South Africa applied. Olga believed if everything were free, the value of what was being offered would be diminished, so they required each participant to contribute or raise 1,000 rand (less than $70) to secure their spot and demonstrate their commitment. For this endeavor, she would be responsible for a diverse group of young and opinionated leaders whom she could help to influence and guide.

Olga was looking for leaders who would return from the trip and effectively spread the word about what they had witnessed, so she did extensive research. Specifically, she tried to learn what drove young Americans to be passionate in their pro-Israel advocacy and realized that there was no one-size-fits-all approach that went into calling oneself a Zionist. All the applicants were type-A leaders in their churches, on social media, or aspiring politicians. She wasn't surprised to learn that the applicants were also deeply familiar with the New Testament, but she was surprised by how many students expressed curiosity and a desire to learn about Israel today.

At the end of the vetting process, she selected twenty-seven Black South African students and leaders between the ages of seventeen and twenty-eight. The group was divided equally between males and females, and there was even one married couple. Some had never been out of the country or even on a plane. They might not have been familiar with Jewish tradition and theology, but they had a deep faith that would immediately create a point of connection with Israelis. Most significantly, they were curious. Those in the more rural parts of the country were interested in Israeli agricultural technology. Some in urban communities were fascinated with the start-up scene and how Israel promoted private sector innovation and entrepreneurship. No matter their area of interest, they all had genuine concerns about how this alleged Israeli apartheid state that they had been taught about would treat them upon their arrival.

Olga had been to Israel before to see the Christian holy sites, but she had never had the responsibility of designing an itinerary. Many Christian denominations across Africa take pilgrimages to see where Jesus walked, but this would be different – the trip would be an attempt to educate the participants about the connection that Jewish people had with their land. They would be able to see it for themselves on the ground and engage in real conversations with diverse Israelis and Palestinians.

But this trip happened when Israel was at war. In response to failed peace talks with Hamas after repeated rocket and mortar fire, the Israel Defense Forces launched Operation Protective Edge on July 8, 2014. They targeted Hamas facilities that were placed in densely populated areas. During the fifty-day conflict, Hamas fired forty-seven hundred rockets and mortars into Israeli cities and towns, some as far as eighty-five miles from Gaza, causing $25 million in damage and putting two-thirds of Israel's civilian population in danger. After a series of short-lived cease-fires, the final cease-fire was agreed upon on August 26, 2014.

During their stay, Olga made sure that she would tackle the biggest and most controversial elephant in the room by showing the realities of the Israeli–Palestinian conflict on the ground. They traveled to Sderot so the group could better understand what it meant to raise children in the shadow of constant rocket attacks. They saw the Golan Heights and looked into the fields of Syria, engulfed by civil war. They had the opportunity to speak with Palestinian Muslims living in the West Bank, where Jews seldom go, and also spoke at length with fellow Christians at a church in Bethlehem. Each night, there was plenty of time set aside for the group to bond and discuss what they had learned that day. It was one thing to read about the land and history in books and online, but it was another to see it firsthand and to meet the people who lived there. For, as curious as this group was about Israel, they couldn't have avoided misinformation, given how mainstream anti-Israel sentiment had become. But each one of their encounters was an opportunity to separate fact from fiction.

One of the most significant lessons occurred at the very beginning of the trip, just after they arrived in Tel Aviv and made their way through customs. Before they even left the airport, the group was introduced to their tour guide for the week, a white Jew, and then boarded the bus to meet their driver for the week: a dark-skinned Muslim. The older participants realized that Israel was not in any way like South Africa during apartheid. In South Africa, that type of professional collaboration would never have occurred.

The trip was a dream come true and exceeded all expectations. Lasting friendships were made, and Olga took special pride in the fact that after this experience, whenever members of the group heard Israel being called an "apartheid state," they would be empowered to speak passionately about why that is both patently false and hurtful to them as Black South Africans, due to what they had witnessed firsthand in Israel.

What Does the Future Have in Store?

The significant role that leaders such as Mandela and Tutu played in the end of apartheid in South Africa is not lost on Olga, even though she strongly disagrees with their views on Israel. Their contribution to the liberation movement cannot be diminished, and Olga is not beyond criticizing Israel when necessary, but she has no tolerance for hypocrisy, and that's what she sees from the BDS movement and anti-Israel faction in her own country. That's why she continues to fight by engaging people and educating them about Israel. Once people start to express curiosity and ask questions, that's when minds can be changed, because so many people just want to do the right thing.

One of the biggest hindrances to Olga's message about Israel is the reality on the ground in South Africa. Many people struggle and are worried about how to feed their families and send their kids to school. Some parts of the country don't have access to basic resources like water. Olga sees how much Israel has to offer the people of South Africa in the form of innovative water and agriculture technology. The question she always poses to those in support of the BDS movement is whether their people should be able to reap the benefits of what a country like Israel has to offer, even if it doesn't align with their political cause. For anyone who truly cares about the welfare of the South African people, the answer has to be yes.

It wasn't long ago that people said South Africa was hopeless, but the people stood together, and the country that emerged after generations of gross inequities exists because of compromise. It is called the Rainbow Nation because it represents people of different skin colors coming together. Apartheid ended, and the new constitution emerged because people who disagreed and had diametrically opposed views sat down and figured out the best solution for the people. Olga's father was a part of that.

Spreading the message is only half the battle. The difficulty comes when trying to get people to speak out and take public action. Even when they have the information, many are scared that BDS or other anti-Israel factions will tear them to pieces or threaten their careers and safety. Olga knows this firsthand. She's been vilified on social media, and people have not wanted to engage with her because of her stance on Israel. Both she and her father have been accused of being paid by Israeli officials using the blood of Palestinians. She's been shouted at and her life has been threatened multiple times. Whenever she speaks publicly in South Africa, she is forced to have personal security – not because she is afraid, but because she knows what her enemies are capable of.

Olga has made amazing friends in the Jewish community, but she's also learned who her friends are. At times, she feels that her work and that of DEISI is not fully embraced and supported across South African Jewry. They encourage her to do what needs to be done, but when she needs their full support, conversations become more difficult. It's been exhausting at times, but she couldn't imagine going back to her family and telling them that she gave up. She could never say that to a man like her father, who, when he saw an injustice being done against Israel, stood up and spoke out. This is in her blood, so if she can't withstand being temporarily unpopular for a good cause, who can?

Today and Tomorrow

The DEISI organization has put its on-the-ground activism on hold for the past two and a half years. God had other plans for Olga, who got married, had a baby, and moved to the United States. She settled in Charlotte, North Carolina, where she began working with an organization called Club Z in January 2020.

The mission of Club Z is to facilitate education and raise a generation of proud and articulate Jewish Zionist high school students. At first, Olga turned down the offer because she didn't understand what she, a non-Jew, could teach American teens about pro-Israel activism. However, the organization kept asking, and Olga realized that as a Black South African woman, she could bring something different to the table. She was in the unique position to show a group of impressionable young students that there were those outside of their community who stood with and loved the Jewish community.

Club Z attempts to educate the younger generation to help them develop a stronger connection with Israel and understand the importance of being a Zionist in the twenty-first century.

Olga continues to do the work she was born to do, and it's not just her family that keeps her going, it's the impact she can make. When she sees the benefit that her people can get from a country like Israel and the beautiful friendships that have been forged across color and faith lines, she knows the struggle has been worth it.

CHAPTER 4

Dragan Primorac
Actively Grateful

At just thirty-eight years old, Dragan Primorac was asked by Prime Minister Ivo Sanader to serve as Croatia's minister of science, education, and sports. It was December 2003, the country was only twelve years old, and as a physician, geneticist, and forensic scientist, Dragan had no government experience, but he had a bold plan to accomplish big dreams.

Having thrived in the American educational system years earlier as a postdoctoral student, Dragan felt that Croatia would benefit from a similar system, so he set out to consolidate the government bureaucracies left over from socialist times. He knew that it would be an uphill battle, but he promised the new prime minister that he would combine the Ministry of Higher Education and the Ministry of Education, for he knew that if Croatia's education system wanted to move forward, it required a seamless and singular ministry.

It wasn't just the American system that inspired Dragan; there was another country that left a significant impression. A small country with a population slightly larger than Croatia, Israel was located in a geopolitically volatile region and constantly under the threat of attack, yet when Dragan first visited in 1998, he discovered a society always open to fostering innovation. Israel was and still is a medical research powerhouse. Dragan's jaw was on the floor when he saw the scope of what was being done in Israel's scientific and academic communities. The country was small but committed to advancing science in every aspect of society. The scientists, researchers, and clinical physicians worked seamlessly together to pioneer in the field of translational medicine.

In 2002, Dragan was introduced to leading venture capitalist and high-tech entrepreneur Nechemia "Chemi" Peres. A pilot in the Israeli Air Force for ten years, Chemi was now the cofounder of Pitango Venture Capital, which he had formed back in 1992. Only seven years older than Dragan, Chemi was also at the start of his career, but had impressed Dragan with his ability to raise over $125 million while simultaneously pioneering in the Israeli venture capitalist community. It was Dragan's first experience with private venture capital and government investment in technology mixing. They spoke at length about the potential for the firm, and as Croatia was rapidly privatizing and its economy growing, Dragan offered to help find deals. That was the beginning of a lasting business and personal relationship. Not only were his horizons being broadened, but Dragan's instincts were spot on; Pitango would go on to become the largest venture capital fund in Israel with $2 billion managed capital by 2016, while Chemi would go on to serve on the boards of several NASDAQ companies and nonprofit organizations.

What Dragan didn't realize in that first meeting was that Chemi was the son of Israeli government leader Shimon Peres, who served twice as prime minister in addition to stints as the minister of foreign affairs, defense, finance, and transportation. Before they parted ways, Chemi promised to organize a meeting between Dragan and Shimon. He followed through on that promise, and the two sat down in December 2002, only a few months after Shimon had left his position as the minister of foreign affairs. That meeting further opened Dragan's eyes about Jewish culture, as well as how Croatia could learn from Israel.

Like Israel, Croatia was forged in war, and Dragan felt that Croatian students should adopt the Israeli method of education. The country's entire curriculum, from kindergarten onward, was focused on innovation and grounded in science. The fledgling government of Croatia needed a big political win to show that the government cared deeply about its students' modern education, so the prime minister encouraged him to pursue the Israeli model if it would allow him to consolidate the bureaucracy.

Dragan didn't stop there. It was a new millennium, and, with the advent of the internet, Croatia needed to adapt to the times, but there wasn't any consensus on where to begin. Dragan felt compelled to go above and beyond his duties as minister to help Croatia gain the world recognition the country craved by showing they were committed to establishing and developing diverse bilateral relations. There was no better way to do that than to invest in the opening of an embassy. He could have suggested they approach some of the bigger allied nations, but instead, he set out to win over the country he admired and wanted to emulate: Israel.

Of all the countries where Israel could open an embassy in a post–Cold War Europe, Croatia was not high on their list. It was small and had a difficult history with antisemitism, particularly certain barbaric atrocities during WWII. When Germany invaded Yugoslavia in 1941, the Independent State of Croatia was created and ruled by a fascist military regime that followed in the footsteps of the Nazi ideology. They created their own laws, and a chain of their own camps where hundreds of thousands of Serbs, Roma, political prisoners, and Jews were sent and killed, most immediately upon arrival. By the end of 1941, many of the country's Jews had been sent to the camps, the most significant being in Jasenovac, which was one of the most notorious in all of Europe. According to noted Israeli historian Gideon Greif, close to one million people were brutally murdered by fifty-seven different methods of killing between 1941 and 1945, which left the Nazis saying that the military fascist regime in Croatia was too bloodthirsty.

Dragan felt that part of being fully respected on the world stage meant taking ownership for what had happened on their soil. The first step was to have honest, open, and continuing dialogue with Israel, a nation formed in response to the horrors of WWII. Only three months into his new job, he was stepping wildly out of his lane, as he wasn't responsible for foreign relations, but he had the blessing of the prime minister.

Education was a priority, and he was committed to modeling the Croatian education system after Israel's. As in many countries, education is mandatory for children in Croatia, but only from ages six to fourteen, so Dragan set out to implement nationwide changes to put students on par with students from other nations. To do that, he felt obligated to deepen existing diplomatic relations. The enormity of the task was not lost on his colleagues, who immediately doubted that his efforts would yield any positive results. Dragan thought the task would be difficult, but not impossible, and he assured his colleagues that some steps had already been made in the right direction.

Israel first recognized the Republic of Croatia in 1992, and full diplomatic relations were established in 1997 and improved significantly when then Croatian president Stjepan Mesic visited Israel in 2001. In 2003, Israeli president Moshe Katsav visited Croatia and left the capital to travel to the Jasenovac concentration camp. He said the trip was difficult and painful, but he was encouraged by the dramatic improvements that had been made in Croatia over the past few years. Although there was very little economic exchange between the two countries, Croatia became an unlikely tourist destination for Israelis around that time. However, it didn't help their burgeoning friendship that Croatia and Iran were courting one another at the time. In May 2003, Croatian foreign minister Tonino Picula had visited Iranian president Mohammad Khatami and encouraged an expansion of international relations and economic cooperation with Israel's sworn enemy.

Dragan's first step to creating an embassy was to reach out to foreign minister and Croatia's recent ambassador to the United States Miomir Žužul to start a dialogue with Yael Rubinstein, the nonresident Israeli ambassador to Croatia. She had a deep understanding of the politics and history of Central and Southeast Europe. Once the introduction was made, Dragan found her to be a wonderful woman. She was quite open to exploring the feasibility of constructing a full embassy in Zagreb, but sober about whether they would receive political approval from the highest levels of Jerusalem. She knew that a budget would be required, which was often hard to find. All Dragan needed to hear was that she was open to the idea. He hadn't gotten used to having a driver yet and was still learning the names of the employees in the ministry building, but he made another in a series of bold – arguably naïve – decisions. He started calling every Israeli he had ever met, aware that they were all in the private sector, and loosely planning a trip for Miomir Žužul, agriculture minister Petar Čobanković, and himself to visit Israel as soon as possible. It would be Dragan's first international trip as a cabinet minister – a title he had held for just four months.

The Croatian press set the bar very high. Since the trip was Dragan's idea, its success would fall on his shoulders. He suspected that some people were hoping this American-educated young maverick would fail; if he did, his short-lived career in public life would end very visibly. It wasn't just the embassy that was at stake; he could be accused of wasting tax dollars on a junket, or it could mean the vocal Israeli press would pile on, too. He was then struck by another thought: since his wife, Jadranka, who served as the economic advisor to the foreign minister, would also be joining the delegation, he realized she might lose her job too if he failed.

The Rise of a Local Statesman

Yugoslavian president Josip Broz Tito helped fight for his country's independence from the Soviet Union after WWII and recognized Israel after the war. The two countries had good relations until 1956, when Tito became an ally of President Nasser of Egypt. After the Six-Day War in 1967, Tito broke off all relations with Israel, and Yugoslavia went so far as to vote for the controversial United Nations resolution equating Zionism with racism.

When Dragan was growing up in Split, Yugoslavia, in the late 1960s and early 1970s, he knew of Israel only as a place of stories from the Bible, since the two countries' ties had been temporarily severed. He knew that Jews used to play an integral role in commerce along the Adriatic Sea. He took pride that the second oldest synagogue in Europe was in the heart of the walled Old City in Dubrovnik, the next city south along the Adriatic. It even had a picturesque alleyway – Zidovska Ulica (Jewish Street). Like everyone in Split, he knew of the old Marjan Hill Cemetery that dated back to the sixteenth century, which had unique letters on some of the seven hundred graves. But these were all just stories, for he had never met any Jewish people as a young man in Marshal Tito's Yugoslavia.

Much changed in those early years, and by the time Dragan graduated from medical school in Split in 1991, his hometown was no longer part of the same country. Yugoslavia no longer existed, and the new country of Croatia was fully immersed in a bloody war. The devastation he witnessed only deepened his commitment to his chosen profession and left him with a strong desire to heal those who had been needlessly wounded while trying to make the world around them a better place. However, resources were limited in Croatia, especially during wartime, so when the opportunity to study in the United States presented itself, Dragan jumped at the chance and settled down in Storrs, Connecticut. Even without the internet or friends who spoke his native language, he achieved what he had set out to do by becoming a postdoctoral fellow and instructor at the University of Connecticut.

Dragan left just in time, for after months of escalating conflict and ethnic tensions between the Catholic Croats and Orthodox Serbs, the president of

Yugoslavia ordered their People's Army (JNA) to create a buffer zone between the two factions after an armed clash at the Plitvice Lakes region of modern-day Croatia on March 31, 1991. A month later, four Croatian policemen tried to replace the Yugoslav flag with Croatia's new flag. When two were captured by the Serbian militia, the conflict quickly escalated. The JNA intervened, but not before twelve Croatian policemen died (some of their bodies were badly mutilated), thus ending any hope for peaceful negotiation. With the six-hour time difference, very little international reporting, and limited phone service, Dragan watched all this unfold from afar.

While he had trained to be a physician and was planning to study the quickly developing field of genetics, he became inspired by three research pioneers who convinced him to change his professional focus to forensics. Dr. Henry Lee had immigrated to the United States from Taiwan twenty years earlier was now the director of the Connecticut State Police Forensic Science Laboratory. He didn't know anyone when he arrived, but thanks to the power of the American educational system, he earned an undergraduate, master's, and a PhD. Professor Moses Schanfield was one of the leading US forensic geneticists, and Dr. Michael Baden was the chief medical examiner for the New York State Police, who had worked in Congress investigating the assassination of JFK. Schanfield and Baden were the first Jews Dragan had ever had a conversation with. They opened Dragan's eyes to how DNA technology could play a critical role at the nexus of criminal justice and medicine. Dragan dove in head first and began training at the Connecticut State Police Forensic Science Laboratory and the Armed Forces Institute of Pathology in Maryland, forever grateful for his academic mentors.

As a bachelor who had the opportunity to travel throughout America, Dragan had a critical life decision to make: return home to a country that no one in America seemed to have heard of, or create a new life away from home.

As he was a citizen of the newly formed country of Croatia, Dragan's three mentors suggested they all put their skills to use there. About a hundred war victims had died in Petrinja between September 1991 and June 1992. Local authorities were able to identify some of the bodies discovered in various mass graves through personal effects, contact lens prescriptions, dental records, earlier bone fractures, and clothing known to the family. But now they could utilize new DNA technology to help identify the remaining bodies. Eager to please and feeling a sense of responsibility to his homeland and his fellow countrymen, Dragan arranged for them to visit the region. They had been the best mentors a young student could have, and it was his obligation to be an equally good host.

Not only had Dragan been away from his family and his home for two years, but he returned to find an almost unrecognizable war-torn landscape, riddled with mass graves and minefields. Heartbreaking stories from neighboring Bosnia had been beamed to households worldwide. He and his colleagues got to work, risking their lives to perform cutting-edge research, because, as scientists, they felt it was their duty. Dragan knew that they were the only ones who would be able to reveal the truth; that meant providing the families of the victims with the closure they needed by identifying the remains of their loved ones, and it also meant revealing who the killers were. If he weren't doing both of those things, he would have felt that he wasn't fulfilling his mission.

They relied on techniques that had been used the previous year to identify the body of Russian Czar Nichols II and his family, who were killed by the Bolsheviks in 1918. They would extract strands of DNA from the bone and teeth and then compare them to the hair and blood samples taken from close relatives to determine a match – a difficult request to make from distraught family members. They were willing to help Croats and Serbs alike identify their dead; it was a duty he felt was more important than any national allegiance. They were not working out of a fully equipped Western laboratory, so it proved to be a tedious job with thousands of steps, which all had to be executed with precision.

During their work, Dragan could not help but see the connection to WWII, and it was his colleagues with deep roots in the Jewish community who started educating him on the horrors of the Holocaust. Of course, he had known about the Holocaust, but after witnessing what happened in his own country and seeing the mass graves out there in the fields, he could suddenly picture the horrific atrocities as if they were unfolding in living color. His Jewish mentors succeeded in helping him fine-tune his professional skill set, but they also helped to change his worldview and broaden his perspective such that he was forever changed by the experience.

In 1995, the bullets finally stopped flying, and that chapter of the bloody Balkan Wars came to an end. He hoped the lab could continue being used in the future to aid in criminal investigations and to detect genetic malformations. Dr. Michael Baden and Dr. Henry Lee returned to America, where they provided expert testimony in the O. J. Simpson murder trial. At a time when so many young and talented professional Croatians were leaving for opportunities in Europe, Australia, or North America, Dragan realized that he wanted to make a life for himself in Croatia, so he settled down in Zagreb. Not yet thirty-five, he had already attracted a lot of media attention and goodwill across Croatia, as his work had been featured in the *New York Times,* the *Chicago Tribune,* and on CNN and NBC. Not only was Dragan making a name for himself, but the public was starting to understand the power of DNA. More importantly, Dragan felt that his work sent a message: nobody could kill innocent people without consequences.

Dragan was bilingual, telegenic, and one of the few medical experts in the country qualified to help foster a curriculum that would educate a new generation of Croatians. Having spent considerable time in the United States, he was also well versed in free-market capitalism, even in the health care sector. It made strong political sense for newly elected prime minister Ivo Sanader to make Dragan a cabinet member.

No Room for Small Dreams

The timing wasn't ideal.

Dragan's planned March 2004 trip to Israel with his fellow cabinet ministers occurred when the country was in turmoil. One month earlier, Israeli prime minister Ariel Sharon had announced the government's incredibly controversial plans to dismantle seventeen Israeli communities in Gaza. That was met with protest and would require the Israeli military to forcibly move its own citizens from their homes. That same month, a suicide bomber affiliated with the Al Aqsa Martyrs Brigade targeted a bus in the heart of Jerusalem. Eight passengers died, and sixty were wounded, many of them children. The tension was somewhat alleviated two Sundays later during the festive Jewish holiday of Purim, but the country was still on high alert and under threat of attack.

In the days leading up to their departure, both Dragan and his wife Jadranka were checking the news constantly. The violence and turmoil promoted a discussion they had never had before, and one they never thought they would have to have: What would happen to their two young daughters if the delegation fell victim to a terrorist attack? But the danger didn't change their resolve. Dragan was committed, and even though Jadranka was scared, she never told him that they shouldn't go.

Dragan was no longer a private citizen. This was his first foray into international diplomacy, and he couldn't help but feel that he was in over his head. Only a few months earlier, he had never dreamed of being in government. His career path was in a white lab coat. The thirty-nine-year-old still hadn't gotten used to having a title and getting people much older than him to follow his directives, yet he was about to sit down with a world leader. He had no idea how he would be received on this stage, and he had no guarantees that all of their efforts to meet with the Israeli leaders would be productive. Perhaps they thought this meeting was just for show, or a five-minute photo op. As they boarded the Croatian government's Bombardier Challenger jet, the scientist in Dragan couldn't help but craft contingency plans; he decided that if it looked like the meeting was turning into a photo op, he'd suggest that the newly elected prime minister of Croatia would personally come to Israel. That could be a way to prolong the meeting and possibly yield some substantial results.

As the jet took off, he tried to relax and enjoy the luxurious first-class accommodations, but his mind was racing. As someone who grew up in a country with a brutal history of antisemitism and who hadn't had a real conversation with a Jew until he arrived in America, he thought of all the Jews he'd met who had helped him forge a deep respect and appreciation for the tiny country that had made such great strides in his academic field.

The view out the window was that of the former Greek, Roman, and Ottoman Empires, all of which sought power and fame in Jerusalem. While looking down at the ancient land, Dragan's mind drifted to the Six-Day War. His Jewish mentors had regaled him more than once with stories of how a much smaller Israel triumphed over the larger Egyptian, Syrian, and Jordanian militaries in June 1967. Specifically, he thought of the great Israeli military leaders of the time – Haim Bar-Lev, the deputy chief of staff of the IDF, raised in Zagreb, and David Elazar, the chief of the Northern Command, born in Sarajevo – who advocated for retaining the Golan. These two Israeli heroes helped to deliver Israel one of the most celebrated victories in military history. It had been rumored that they would often communicate in Croatian to disguise their correspondence from the enemy and their own junior officers. Dragan never met either man, yet he felt connected to them because they came from the same place.

Once on the ground at Ben-Gurion International Airport, the delegation was met by a motorcade that took them at rapid speed to Jerusalem's David Citadel Hotel, where they arrived in well under an hour. Before they even set foot on the street, their Israeli security detail rushed them out of the car, around the building, and through the kitchen. They were less than one-quarter of a mile away from where the bus bombing had been, and the threat remained very real, so the delegation always entered the hotel through a different entrance and never through the front lobby. Dragan knew of the danger in the area, but the level of security considered necessary was still an eye-opener. He joked with his wife about the uniqueness of Israeli hospitality, but they were both grateful that precautions were being taken.

Their first scheduled meeting was on Sunday, March 14, with Prime Minister Ariel Sharon, who, after the Croatian prime minister, would only be the second world leader Dragan had ever met. Upon their arrival, the delegation was led into a room where the flags of both countries were on display in the middle of a large table. He started to run through all the different scenarios in his head. Then he saw coffee laid out and realized gratefully that it would be more than a five-minute affair.

Pleasantries were exchanged. Dragan shook hands with Prime Minister Sharon, and even though he towered over the short, stout former general, he felt dwarfed by the man's accomplishments. "I understand that you are Croatia's top scientist and an expert on genetics," said Sharon as they settled into their seats. "Can you tell me about the origin of modern man and how old the world is?"

Caught off guard by the question, Dragan tensed up. That was the last thing on his mind, but Dragan had published an article about the origins of European man four years earlier. He knew that evolution was a sensitive subject, and he had no idea how religious Prime Minister Sharon and the other Israelis around the table might be. Trying to think of a way to play it safe, he was about to launch into an explanation when the prime minister burst out laughing. It was a much-needed icebreaker that put Dragan at ease for the first time all day.

What followed happened quickly. Prime Minister Sharon stood up and started the meeting by announcing Israel's intention to open an embassy in Zagreb. Just like that, Dragan's dream had come true, and his first diplomatic mission was accomplished. Like Dragan, the others in the Croatian delegation were shocked, and it took a moment for them to register what had happened. Their new friend Yael Rubinstein gave them a smile and a nod on the far side of the table before going back to furiously taking notes. Sharon continued by offering to launch a strategic science and technology partnership that would allow for regular exchanges of academics, business leaders, and policymakers.

Outside, political history was being made, and the future of the Sharon government was in doubt, but the prime minister remained calm and cordial. He was unfazed by the domestic unrest and the daily chaos happening all around him. The Croatian delegation had his undivided attention, and Dragan was blown away by his poise. Unsure if he would be able to do the same in his shoes, he made a mental note of the lesson in leadership he was watching unfold before his eyes.

After all the pressure from his fellow cabinet members, late nights spent monitoring the news in Israel, and coming up with scenarios for how to respond if Israel didn't take his request seriously, he could finally breathe a sigh of relief. With the high-octane geopolitics and security concerns in their rearview mirror, Dragan and the delegation had the chance to be tourists in between their other meetings and appearances. They visited the Roman ruins in the ancient port city of Caesarea. When looking out at the city built by King Herod between 22 and 10 BCE, he was reminded of his childhood back in Split, a tourist destination and ancient Roman vacation spot.

Before they returned home, they were treated to a round of golf at the Caesarea Golf Club with Dragan's friend Moti Giladi, an Israeli actor and singer. Built in 1961, it was the first course in the Middle East. Even though they appreciated the gesture, neither Dragan nor anyone in the Croatian delegation had ever held a club, never mind understood the rules of golf. Dragan had already defied the odds, so he wouldn't turn down a challenge. As his country's sports minister, he felt somewhat obliged. When he stepped to the first tee and took his first-ever swing of a golf club, he hit the longest drive of the group – a memory that fully cemented his love for Israel and his hosts.

Dragan learned that the Israeli government had been afraid the Croatians would postpone their visit for security reasons. The fact that they did choose to pursue this opportunity, so soon after the Croatian elections, less than fifteen years into being an independent country, and during one of Israel's tensest times, clearly left an impression on Jerusalem's political elite.

Diplomatic Influence

After the round of golf, the delegation was entertained that night at a club, where Dragan was exposed to a different side of Israeli hospitality. He was surprised to learn that the waiters, bartenders, and everyday Israelis knew a lot about Croatia. The more he spoke with them, the more he realized that much of that knowledge stemmed from his country's impressive third-place finish at the 1998 World Cup in France, no small feat for such a tiny nation less than a decade old. He experienced jealousy from proud fans of Israeli soccer, but, reading between the lines, he realized this was an opportunity to connect.

Those conversations got Dragan thinking about his next venture, so he got to work arranging a friendly soccer match between the Israeli national team and Croatia as soon as he returned to Zagreb. He got it on the schedule for November 2004, but it was not sanctioned by UEFA. In February 1999, they had enforced a two-year ban allegedly for security concerns, so the match attracted a lot of eye rolls and outright scorn from the international soccer community. Dragan knew that if anything happened to his country's beloved soccer players while they were in Israel, he would become a national disgrace. The game ended in a 3–3 tie, but they made it home safely, and it proved to be another step forward in diplomatic relations between the two countries.

It wasn't all smooth sailing, though. For example, Croatia hosted Iranian president Mohammad Khatami – the leader of a country whose government officials frequently referred to Israel as "Little Satan" – in March 2005. Later that same year, the hardline mayor of Tehran, Mahmoud Ahmadinejad, was elected to replace Khatami, and he began to say Israel must be "wiped off the map." With such open hostility, ongoing relations with Iran didn't help Croatia's attempt to get in Israel's good graces, yet Dragan was not deterred. He encouraged all of his fellow ministers not to neglect their burgeoning friendship with Israel. Much as Dragan had intuited upon his return to Croatia back in 1993, the most significant strides were made when the country was forced to come to terms with its own brutal past. When Croatian president Stjepean Mesíc traveled to Israel in 2005, he met with the Simon Wiesenthal Center's Israel director, Dr. Efraim Zuroff, to discuss the prosecution of Nazi-era war criminals in the former Yugoslavia in order to help aid in the postwar reconciliation process.

Dragan would make multiple trips to Israel, and finally, he saw his dream come to fruition when Israel opened its embassy in Zagreb on Monday

September 8, 2005. It was a feather in his cap, but his work wasn't done. Two years later, he hosted Israel's Vice Premier Shimon Peres, in his hometown at the beautiful Hotel Le Meridien Lav, and together they formally launched a joint Israeli–Croatian science fund. When speaking to the press, Dragan said that he believed Peres deserved to become president of Israel, and two months later, on July 15, 2007, that was exactly what happened. When Shimon Peres was sworn in as the Israeli president, Dragan was one of the few invited international guests to the family's inauguration dinner.

Never one to think small, Dragan went above and beyond his duties as education minister to help forge the alliance between Croatia and Israel. Having accomplished everything that he set out to do and much more, he decided to leave the cabinet in January 2009 and return to private life, but his influence continues to be felt.

Today, 164 nations recognize Israel, but because of Dragan's diligent efforts, Croatia – a country with only four million citizens – is one of only sixty-nine locations worldwide with an Israeli embassy and resident ambassador. He may no longer serve in government, but he continues to develop Croatia's ties to Israel as the founder and honorary president of the Croatian–Israeli Business Club. Each month, Dragan endeavors to advance cooperation between the two countries and build on their robust collaboration in the fields of energy, tourism, health, agriculture, education, and technology.

After over two hundred meetings with business, academic, and government leaders, Dragan made a lifetime of memories, but very little compares to those four days he spent in Israel back in 2004, and the victory he celebrated at the country club after his first-ever diplomatic adventure.

CHAPTER 5
Gloria and Jose Garcés
Faithfully Bold

Music and faith have always played a significant part in the lives of Gloria and Jose Garcés. They inherited that from their parents, who met in Guatemala after fleeing Castro's Cuba. Their father, a former civil engineer, devoted his life to faith and built innovative churches. He found a way to blend both passions by starting One Voice Records, which became the second-largest Spanish-language Christian record label in the world. When the Garcéses emigrated to Miami just before Christmas 1988, the diverse and talented family of eight filled the niche of Spanish gospel music in the land of opportunity. Helping the church grow became a family affair, and everyone contributed. Their mother, a recording artist and singer, led the way. She may have been shy and reserved, but she came alive when singing. Soon, all of the children were dancing and playing instruments – Jose played the drums and Gloria the flute. Verbo Church rapidly grew and became one of the premier evangelical Spanish-speaking churches in Florida.

Gloria was four and a half years older than Jose, and the siblings read and taught each other the Bible from a very young age. As they got older, biblical stories became a popular topic of conversation, not just every Sunday during church, but at the dinner table, so the children each became well versed in the life of Jesus.

While growing up in Miami, Gloria made many Jewish friends. They taught her Hebrew songs, and when she was twelve, she took Israeli dance classes. She was exposed to an entirely different culture and quickly became fascinated with the Holy Land. She'd return home and teach her family about Moses's sister, Miriam, who danced, sang, and played the tambourine during the parting of the Red Sea. Gloria's obsession would remain with her into adulthood and inspire her to attempt things that others would think impossible – things that could change the geopolitical landscape.

The Seed Is Planted

In 1948, Guatemala became one of the first Central American countries to recognize Israel, and Guatemalan ambassador to the UN Jorge García Granados actively lobbied other countries to recognize the Jewish state, which led fourteen other nations to support the November 1947 United Nations partition plan. Granados would go on to become Guatemala's first ambassador to Israel. It's no surprise that Jerusalem and many towns in Israel have a Guatemala Street. Antisemitism is rare, and schools prioritize Holocaust education.

Before 1980, Guatemala and many other countries had embassies in Jerusalem, but Israel passing a law identifying Jerusalem as its "indivisible and eternal capital" led the UN Security Council to call on Guatemala and several other countries to move their embassies to Tel Aviv – just one of the many decisions that contributed to the UN's outsized role in Israel. After Yom Haatzmaut (Israeli Independence Day) in May 2017, Prime Minister Benjamin Netanyahu called for Israel's allies to move their embassies back to Jerusalem.

Gloria's fascination with Israel did not wane in adulthood, and she closely watched the country's events unfold from her home in Miami. She knew that Israel and Guatemala had pledged to create a more profound friendship in recent years. During a 2016 state dinner at which Israeli president Reuven Rivlin hosted the Guatemalan president, Rivlin referred to Guatemala and

Israel as "partners in action." Prime Minister Netanyahu made Israel's interest in Latin America clear with his plans to modernize water and agriculture technology for the benefit of the Guatemalan people. However, Gloria boldly thought this burgeoning relationship could go a step further: she hoped that Israel could forge an even tighter bond with her home country by having Guatemala be the first to open an embassy in Jerusalem.

As a busy, divorced mother of fifteen-year-old Sofia, Gloria already had a full plate, but she knew how to make room for a cause close to her heart. Media savvy and well connected in the Latino and Jewish communities of South Florida, she felt the key was to use her resources to get a personal meeting with Guatemalan president Jimmy Morales. A former actor and comedian who was elected only a year earlier in 2016, Morales also had a connection to Israel, having traveled there to receive an honorary doctorate from Hebrew University just after being elected president. Guatemala was a country with fewer than eighteen million people, and with her vast international network of high-profile connections, Gloria felt it was only a matter of time before she found someone close to President Morales. Even if it was only his barber, Gloria was confident she could talk her way into a meeting, and once in the room, there was no doubt that she could convince the president to open a Jerusalem embassy.

There was one group of people that she could rely on for support no matter what the problem: her family. If anything, they all shared the same bold ability to dream big, so they understood the scope of her ambitions. Her family helped to create a Christian music category at the Latin Grammy Awards, which took two years of lobbying and strategic public relations. If they could navigate the bureaucracy of the Grammys, they could get Guatemala to move an embassy.

The first person she called was her brother.

Jose had moved back to Guatemala in 2005 to join his parents, who had returned a year earlier and opened a series of restaurants unlike any other in the country. The flagship was Nais Aquarium Restaurant, which was home to hundreds of fish, including stingrays and moray eels. A scuba diver would put on feeding shows for the customers multiple times a day, and every child wanted a birthday there, so customers flocked to the restaurant. With a son and two daughters of his own, Jose soon found himself immersed in the family business.

It was another busy night at the restaurant in May 2017 when Jose got a frantic call from Gloria. He tried to tell her that he would call her back at a better time, but she insisted that he grab their father and retreat to the office. She had something to discuss that couldn't wait.

At first, he feared the worst, but he knew his sister well enough to recognize the excitement in her voice. She had another one of her big ideas, and he knew better than anyone that she wouldn't take no for an answer, so he wrangled his father away from a discussion with some of the restaurant's regular patrons and went back to the office to put Gloria on speaker phone. "I don't know how, but we need to get President Morales to move the Guatemalan embassy from Tel Aviv to Jerusalem. Guatemala can lead the world and be number one!"

Neither Jose nor his father was political, so they weren't familiar with the thorny geopolitics of the United Nations or the significance of where the building was located, but Gloria's passion and determination were infectious as usual. Jose and Gloria both knew the Bible, but it was through his sister that Jose developed an understanding of modern-day Israel and its connection to Guatemala. "Let me sleep on it," Jose told his sister. It wasn't a question of whether or not he supported her plan; it was about figuring out how he could help.

Gloria didn't wait. Excited and a bit naïve, she pressed on. Her next phone call was to a friend in Los Angeles who she thought might be friends with the president's brother. The call went nowhere. She sat down and tried to develop a plan, which began in her own backyard. Florida is home to one of the largest Jewish communities in the world, so she picked up the phone and tried to put out feelers. But every person she talked to gave a different version of the same answer: "It's impossible." "It's diplomatically incorrect." "It's political suicide."

Gloria refined the plan once again, and instead of the long shot of hoping someone she knew might be able to put her in touch with President Morales, she decided to leverage the diplomatic connections she already had. That's when she reached out to Consul General Lior Haiat, the top Israeli diplomat serving the Southeast United States out of Miami. When Gloria laid out her plan, Haiat broke out in laughter. It was a response she was getting used to, but it only made her more dedicated to the cause. She told Haiat, "I am getting a meeting with President Morales within a month. I need to know what

Israel is going to bring to the table." Even though he admired her gusto, he felt the decision to move the embassy was above his pay grade and wished her the best of luck.

The people she talked to couldn't do anything for her, and, more than that, the way her request was being received made her think that she might need more help executing her idea.

The Torch Is Passed

After giving it some thought, Jose was fully on board. He started with some of the Jewish parents at his son's private school. The Guatemalan Jewish community was small, but tight-knit and well connected. But Jose's luck wasn't much better than Gloria's, so he and his father went back to the drawing board and came up with another plan, which utilized what the family did best.

The restaurants gave them access to a venue and available food, and years of commitment to the religious community had helped them create a rapport with some of the most respected faith leaders in the country. Instead of attempting to find the needle in the haystack that might lead them to President Morales, they decided to use their network to stir up support by hosting regular meetings. During their first gathering, they talked about the unity of the church, their country's relationship with Israel, and the importance of the embassy. They quoted Scripture about Jerusalem, made new friends, and took old friendships to a new level. That first event stirred up so much interest that it wasn't long before they were hosting meetings every Tuesday and Thursday. Jose and his father set aside space at various restaurants across Guatemala City and had their chefs put together leftovers from the kitchens to provide plenty of food. Their grassroots effort worked, and they quickly met a pastor who was confident he could get the Garcés family a meeting with President Morales.

As in many countries, it was common in Guatemala for politicians to go to church – especially before an election. But it was unprecedented to bring the voices of thousands of congregants to influence public policy. The clergy and their congregants never thought this an option until American-educated Jose began talking about his family's plan. Together, they were beginning to see how the system could work and that they could, in fact, affect the change they desired. Jose had never touched politics before, but Gloria's bold dream inspired him to begin thinking of the many possibilities available.

With a face-to-face sit-down with the president on the horizon, Gloria took a personal vacation from work and traveled with her daughter down to Guatemala. She remained confident in her powers of persuasion and prepared diligently for the meeting. She rehearsed talking points with the pastor who had made the arrangements. On the day of the meeting, they received a note from the president's chief of staff informing them that the president would not be able to attend due to recent schedule changes. He suggested that the foreign minister would hear out their proposal and take any recommendation seriously.

A trip that began with such promise ended with Gloria getting the cold shoulder, but she was going to make sure that it wasn't a complete waste of time. She chose instead to bond with her daughter by doing something she had been meaning to do for thirty years. They spent five hours hiking up Mount Pacaya, an active volcano at 8,400-foot elevation. The ground was so hot that they stopped and roasted marshmallows. When life gave Gloria lemons, she always found a way to make lemonade.

Gloria tried to keep her spirits high, but she couldn't help but wonder if everyone who doubted her was right. She had already exhausted most of her contacts and saw for the first time that the odds were heavily stacked against her. Guatemala was not being formally asked by Israel to move their embassy, so there was no pressure on the government to even address the issue. Why would the Guatemalan Ministry of Foreign Affairs want to take the time and spend the money required to move into a new embassy? More significantly, why would they want to rock the boat and potentially risk the ire of the entire Muslim world when they already had a functioning embassy in Tel Aviv?

Once back in Miami, Gloria considered throwing in the towel and forgetting her short-lived dream.

Let's Harmonize Guatemala

Whatever motivation Gloria might have lost was gained tenfold by Jose, who became more determined than ever to, in their words, "establish an altar to publicly worship the God of Israel." Always having a bold, innovative mind, Jose pivoted and decided to utilize the family's other passion: music. Before leaving the United States for Guatemala over a decade earlier, Jose had helped the family establish and then sell their record label to Grammy Award–winner Bob Carlisle in Nashville. Although he was now out of the music industry, he had remained in touch with his old colleagues and started working the phones.

It became clear right away that he hadn't been forgotten, for he received a tremendous amount of support. He quickly put together a team of fifteen of his old friends, who began working on planning a massive demonstration of faith in the Plaza de la Constitución. Everyone did their part, and they called in favors to secure the requisite permits – no easy task, since staging an event (especially one with state-of-the-art speakers and lighting) in the plaza was equivalent to getting permission to put on a performance in front of the White House, but they needed to be visible to all the government officials they wanted to influence. Jose was going to put the God of Israel right on the doorstep of President Morales. Armonicemos Guate was the name they decided on for the event, which translates to "Let's Harmonize Guatemala."

People donated their money and their time. That summer, Jose hosted weekly meetings at his restaurant, many going late into the night, and they were able to secure the permission and permits necessary to hold the gathering on Saturday, August 19, 2017. With only a couple of weeks to put everything together, they wasted no time booking some of the top Latin Christian acts. Having spent considerable time in the music business, Jose was worried that egos might be an issue when it came to billing, so he insisted that no advertising mention the performers themselves: the focus was to be entirely on the message. They wouldn't even have an emcee; the donated microphones would only be used for musical acts and for historic group prayer. It wasn't all that surprising that some of the more prominent names in music backed out, but Jose was able to convince a few of the local faith leaders to take their place.

Just like his sister, Jose was a visionary and dreamer who always shot for the stars. It wasn't just about the performers; it was about the spectacle in the plaza. He wanted drummers, guitarists, and brass musicians – twenty-one hundred musicians total and four thousand more volunteers all wearing donated white T-shirts with the seventy-two names of God written on them.

After one Thursday night meeting at their restaurant, a Baptist pastor needed a ride back to his church. Jose joked about being used for a ride, but he and his father gave the man a lift and were invited inside the church. Jose was reluctant because he was dressed in jeans and sneakers, but he went in anyway and was glad he did, because they happened to see President Jimmy Morales and a few congressmen worshiping right there in the building. Jose and his father knew that it was a sign, so they stayed for the service and introduced themselves to the president and his contingent afterward. Before

Jose could diplomatically bring up the event he was planning and the future of the embassy, his father blurted out, "What happened a few weeks ago when you canceled on my daughter? When are we talking about the embassy in Israel?"

That line of questioning didn't get them anywhere with the president, who left soon afterward, but a few congressmen stayed behind to learn what this embassy discussion was all about. Jose learned that the government – seemingly in a state of panic and disarray at this point – needed to postpone the event a week to August 26. Jose rolled with the punches and quickly got back to work with his team, coordinating with all the musicians and faith leaders. Not only did none of the acts back out, but they were able to arrange buses from El Salvador, Mexico, and Honduras that would transport worshipers to what was shaping up to be a historic event.

But just as everything was coming together, it seemed the Guatemalan government was unraveling. Controversy surrounded the president and, in response, protestors attempted to co-opt months of work by the Garcés family and utilize the platform for their own demonstration against Morales. When the volunteers set up the stage on Friday evening, the media came out in full force to film the demonstration, and Jose had to intervene. He somehow managed to convince the media to put down their cameras and join him in prayer. Afterwards, he explained how what was happening the next day was neither pro- nor anti-government: it was a collective worship of the God of Israel as well as a celebration of Guatemala's history of supporting Israel.

Despite Jose's best efforts, rumors continued to swirl about twenty thousand anti-government protestors descending on the plaza. Jose heard that many believed those rumors had been started by the foreign minister. The fear of potential riots caused musicians to grow nervous and some to back out. Only three hundred of the twenty-one hundred musicians showed up, and, to add insult to injury, it began to rain that fateful Saturday.

Jose and his team had experienced setback after setback after setback. When faced with another set of challenges, they turned to what had helped them endure every obstacle up to that point: prayer. Despite everything, when Armonicemos Guate started, worries and problems were forgotten; people didn't even seem to notice the light rain or the anti-government protestors. Crowds cheered the musical acts, and everyone celebrated. It was a magical spectacle that even Jose couldn't have envisioned.

When the music stopped at 6:18 p.m. as planned, the sun seemed to stand still as it approached the horizon. It took about seven minutes for all of the prayer teams at each intersection to make their way to the plaza. It was such a powerful and emotional moment that even the protestors stood down and joined in on the worship. And right then, at the climax of the event, the country of Guatemala experienced a small earthquake. Like everyone in attendance, Jose felt a brief jolt of fear and uncertainty, but as the ground stopped shaking, he knew that everything was happening just as it should. They were not going to fail in their mission, because what he had just experienced was a sign.

That night, Jose stayed behind with the crew as they broke down the stage. He knew they still had a long way to go to achieve their goal, but he personally thanked the organizers for their support nevertheless and did his best to make sure to congratulate as many people as he could for making his dream project a success. As the night wound down, all he wanted to do was go home and go to bed, but his father convinced him to attend a dinner that night with Efraín, the vice president's chief of staff. He was glad he did attend, because Jose found an ally for their cause. "Israel is very close to my heart," Efraín said to Jose. "My daughter lives there and is studying medicine." The more Jose listened to Efraín talk, the more he realized how much impact Armonicemos Guate had made. The senior government officials might not have been there on the stage or in the crowd, but they watched the show from their office fortress only a few hundred feet away. And Jose knew that anybody who witnessed what happened that day felt its impact.

A few days later, Jose learned the real power of government influence when Efraín introduced him to the brand-new foreign minister, Sandra Jovel. She was just thirty-eight and, like Jose, an Evangelical Protestant. She was deeply religious and shared Jose's passion and vision. They immediately hit it off. The die was cast, and together they began devising a plan to make Gloria's once far-fetched dream to move the Guatemalan embassy from Tel Aviv to Jerusalem a reality.

History in the Making

For someone who had had no interest in politics only a few months earlier, Jose got a crash course in government bureaucracy. Ironically, only then did he begin to see how challenging the task he and his sister had set out to achieve actually was, yet he was even more committed to seeing this through to the end. It soon became a full-time job.

Jose remained in frequent contact with Sandra Jovel and continued to host meetings with church leaders every Tuesday and Thursday. As they moved closer to their goal, he adapted the meetings accordingly. He realized the support he had received from the community was more spiritual than practical and that the church community was united regardless of denomination. But even though the people knew their Bible inside and out, they weren't nearly as familiar with the modern realities of Israel or the significance of their goal of moving the embassy. To many of them, Israel was the place they read about on Sunday, but it was starting to come to life as Jose helped them to better understand the Holy Land's people, customs, and connection to Guatemala's own past.

By December 2017, Jose had hosted over four hundred meetings and, even though he and Gloria never wanted anything more than to find favor in God's eyes, he was exhausted. Feeding twenty-five people a couple of times a week was taking its toll, as were the hours he had spent trying to hammer home the same talking points. Just when hope began to fade, Gloria phoned Jose with some bad news: no longer would Guatemala be the first country to move its embassy to Jerusalem. The United States made its own announcement on December 6. But the news was invigorating, and neither Gloria nor Jose was deterred. If anything, they pushed harder, for that was in their blood, and it was all they knew. As fate would have it, their efforts paid off most unexpectedly.

On Christmas Eve that same year, Sandra Jovel was one of the Guatemalan leaders present when President Morales spoke on the phone with Israeli prime minister Benjamin Netanyahu. After pleasantries were exchanged, Morales went off script and shocked everyone in the room by saying he was making arrangements to go forward with the embassy move.

Gloria was spending Christmas at her sister's house in Tallahassee, Florida. She tried to put her efforts related to the embassy away and focus on family for the holiday. They had just eaten dinner and opened a few presents when Gloria noticed she had missed five calls from Jose. Before she even had a chance to call him back, Jose tried her again and broke the news. It took a moment for her to process the information, but once she finally did, she broke out into the first Israeli dance she had learned as a child. When she finally calmed down, Gloria called the Israeli consul general, Lior, the government official who had felt that the embassy move was above his pay grade, and jokingly asked him, "Who is laughing now?" He had yet to hear the news and at first couldn't believe it, but congratulated Gloria on her follow-through.

What began as a pipe dream for Gloria became official when President Morales posted the announcement on Facebook later that night. Once word got out, everyone tried to take credit. Pro-Israel and Jewish-American leaders were rushing to meet with President Morales and Foreign Minister Jovel to make headlines for themselves and their organizations. Jose frequently got calls from Jovel asking if he knew the people who were contacting them.

The Garcés family had learned how to move fast, so they suggested that the president and foreign minister host a well-publicized visit in January for Jewish community and faith leaders traveling from the United States. It proved to be the first and only time that kosher food was served by the Guatemalan government. The full cabinet joined the dinner along with evangelical leaders from across Latin America and politically active Jewish leaders worldwide. But even after the announcement, and having their contribution acknowledged by the country's leadership, it didn't feel real.

There Are No Coincidences

Gloria and her daughter traveled to Israel to witness history when President Morales and Prime Minister Netanyahu were to dedicate a new embassy of Guatemala in Jerusalem on May 16, 2018 – two days after the United States had moved their embassy.

After checking in to the David Citadel Hotel, she stood on the terrace by the pool that overlooked the walls of the Old City. She kept thinking about the Bible verses she had learned as a girl and of the challenges Jesus faced. She felt chills when she saw the flags of Guatemala, Israel, and the United States proudly beamed on the walls that night through large light displays. Those same flags were on display all over the city the next morning as she traveled to the embassy for the ceremony, along with giant billboards reading, "Thank you!" in English, Spanish, and Hebrew.

Being there on the ground in Jerusalem and seeing those three flags side by side put the enormity of the task she had been working so hard to achieve in perspective. The United States may have been first, but it has a GDP many times that of Guatemala. The United States may have overshadowed

Guatemala on the international stage, but for that one week, the two countries shared the same vision and were on equal footing. It was humbling for Gloria to think of the role she had played in helping the country of her birth make history in the country that was deeply in her heart, and to do it alongside her adopted country was even more remarkable.

The offices were still under construction and far from complete, but eighty guests and international press crammed into the tiny reception room with the two world leaders. Gloria found herself just a few feet away from Morales and Netanyahu as the ribbon was cut. With unmistakable joy, Gloria saw these world leaders take a small piece of the blue-and-white ribbon and use it as a pocket square.

This was the moment the family had fought to achieve for so long, and it still felt surreal even though Gloria watched it all unfold before her eyes. Surrounded by billionaires, rabbis, Guatemalan elected officials, and world media, she had to pinch herself. The past year had been a whirlwind, but the world had finally slowed down, and reality sunk in for Gloria when she was asked to take a photo of the entire group. Jose was in the back of the room, the rest of the family was off to the side, and the faces of the many people who had helped out were scattered throughout the room. Suddenly, she realized that all eyes were focused on her, even the world leaders, and time stood still for a brief moment as she snapped the picture that journalists from around the globe would later ask her for. When time resumed, it hit her all at once. Other than the birth of her daughter, it was the happiest moment of her life.

Gloria wanted to find Jose, but she was asked at the last minute to serve as the translator for the Guatemalan First Lady. What she didn't know was that her services were being requested for a private conversation between the First Lady and Sara Netanyahu. It was the first time the two powerful women ever met, and Gloria was privy to the whole thing.

The night ended with a cocktail party for over three hundred guests, hosted by the Guatemalan delegation at the King David Hotel. After a monumental day for both Israel and Guatemala, she was finally able to have a private moment of reflection and prayer with Jose and their family. There is no word in the Bible for *coincidence*, and the two siblings firmly believe that everything that had happened in the last year did so for a reason. There was a reason the family had left the music industry and gone into the restaurant business, for, without that, they wouldn't have been able to win over the faith leaders and their congregants who helped them build a persuasive grassroots movement.

In one year, Jose and Gloria Garcés had gone from everyday citizens to being part of high-stakes geopolitics and diplomacy. They had been in different countries, but they had gone to battle together, and their contributions helped make history. It seemed fitting that they shared that moment in the King David Hotel, a hotel that had witnessed so much history in a holy city whose history dates back thousands of years.

CHAPTER 6
Joan Ryan
Authentically Prudent

On a cold, overcast Tuesday in February 2019, Joan Ryan made what she called the most consequential decision of her life. After three decades of service, she resigned from the United Kingdom's Labour Party. She felt she had no choice, and she wasn't alone: she was the eighth member of Parliament (MP) to quit in just forty-eight hours.

After posting a four-page resignation letter on Twitter laying out her position, she knew that she was about to face a media blitz. By dawn, satellite trucks were outside her suburban London home. Print and radio reporters were eagerly waiting for a statement. She knew what she was doing; during a press conference for Sky News in front of a nearby hospital, she was not subtle about saying that the Labour Party should return to being focused on the lack of primary care doctors in the UK instead of attacking their own MPs for ideological differences.

When the interviews were over, she boarded the commuter train to the center of London with her aide, just as she did every other workday, but that train ride was the longest of her career. Surrounded by working-class constituents, she couldn't help but reflect on her life in politics and how she had fought for those same commuters, day in and day out.

The eyes of every Westminster staffer, police officer, journalist, and colleague were on Joan when she entered the parliament building at 11:45 a.m. and passed through the metal detectors. Here, she wasn't a stranger. Everyone had seen the interviews from a few hours earlier. Once in the House of Commons Chambers, it hit her that she had reached the end of the line politically. She could see the good friends and colleagues she had sat with for years, but protocol would not allow her to sit with them. It was bittersweet, but she felt that a tremendous weight had been lifted. She was welcomed instead by a small group of women who had left the Conservative Party.

It was no longer "just politics." The ostracization of Joan was only the beginning. In the weeks that followed, many of the younger colleagues she had mentored wanted nothing to do with her. One of her female protégés, with whom she regularly had pizza, said they could get together, but only if it were late at night and in a location where they wouldn't run into anyone.

Joan had essentially thrown away her professional life's work, but she had no regrets. She felt more powerful than she had in years. Doing the right thing was its own reward, but she never would have thought, even five years earlier, that her commitment to Israel and the Jewish people would lead to her political downfall.

Stories from the Survivors

Raised Catholic by Irish immigrants in the then predominantly Protestant England, Joan knew about adversity from a young age. When she gave birth to her son at the age of nineteen, she was forced to grow up quickly. She worked a series of odd jobs until age twenty-four, when she moved to London and enrolled in a master's program with the help of funding from the Inner London Education Authority. Four years later, she gave birth to her second child. She was a single mother trying to juggle the demands of two little ones at home when she began teaching teenagers at the public school.

In 1985, Joan was approached by a friend who worked full-time at the Imperial War Museum as an oral historian. The museum was looking for freelancers to interview various subjects and would pay £48 per recorded hour. A teacher's salary was low, and she wanted to use the extra money to move into a new apartment so that her kids could each have a bedroom. After school, her mother, who had moved to London as a widow, started watching the kids while Joan conducted interviews. She worked late hours and was gone most of the day, but always made sure to be home in time to put the kids to bed.

The museum leased out recording equipment and gave her dossiers on various WWII veterans and Bevin Boys, conscripted miners often called the "forgotten" wartime workforce, whom she was scheduled to interview. Each interview took about twelve hours; they were held in the homes of the different subjects. Over a couple of days, she got to know many of them very well, and they often asked her to stick around for tea, wanting to chat. She was only getting paid for the recorded time, so any time outside of the interview was cutting into time with her family, but she still found it difficult to turn down a friendly invitation.

On the anniversary of the day Auschwitz was liberated, Joan read a profile of Freddie Knoller in the *Hendon & Finchley Times*, a local newspaper in an area of London with a large Jewish community. Freddie was a Holocaust survivor who was fourteen and living in Vienna on Kristallnacht and later moved to London in 1947. The story impacted her so much that she suggested to her bosses that she begin interviewing Holocaust survivors on behalf of the museum. They agreed, as long she could find subjects who were willing to talk. In her free time, Joan used the Imperial War Museum records to research the Holocaust and do all her own prep work. Not having grown up around many Jews and knowing only about the religion and post-WWII community secondhand, she quickly gained an entirely different perspective about WWII and London's tight-knit Jewish community. Once thoroughly prepared, she phoned Freddie first, and he was eager to do a formal interview.

From that very first interview, Joan knew that she was doing significant work. Freddie was not a well-known leader in the Jewish community, he was just a person trying to live out the rest of his life. As soon as he started opening up, she was riveted. Not wanting casual banter or interjections to make their way onto the tape, she maintained eye contact and made sure to only smile and nod. He revealed details to Joan that he had never even told his family. By the time he finished telling his story, she had almost twenty-four hours of recorded footage.

Joan's interview with Freddie was well received, and he helped her locate other Holocaust survivors. Some had endured Auschwitz, Bergen-Belsen, and Dachau. She even spoke to some of the Windermere Boys, who were sent to live in England after the concentration camps were liberated, and a woman who had been on a death march from Lithuania. Every story and interview subject was unique, but they all shared some common yet unexpected qualities. It wasn't just what they endured, but their incredible resilience in coping with what they witnessed that inspired Joan. The experience of being there in the house, face-to-face with the person, was so different from merely reading a story or profile. For the interviewees to relive it all right in front of her made her feel like an active participant who, in her search for more detail, served as a guide through this very personal and not-so-distant history.

When promoted at the school she taught at in 1988, Joan was given a pay increase, and with that came more responsibility. She had to cut back on her time at the museum, but her work there left a lasting impression on her. The unbelievable opportunity to document those stories for the national archive was a cathartic and emotional experience that helped solidify her understanding of her own values and principles.

Standing Up for the Oppressed

What Joan witnessed in her own community started to change the way she looked at things. She admired how people helped each other out and stuck together. She thought of her upbringing – how her immigrant parents faced adversity but worked hard to help their kids achieve something better. Never interested in politics growing up, Joan began to feel a responsibility to give a voice to underrepresented communities who didn't realize they could speak up in the British democratic system. She believed that the philosophy and mindset were at the core of the Labour Party, and she was elected as a local counselor for the East Finchley ward in 1990. Her rise in the party was swift. In 1997, she was elected Labour member of Parliament for Enfield North for the first of five times and would later serve as assistant whip under Tony Blair from 2002 to 2006.

Enfield North was home to the Forty Hall Vineyard, the Tottenham Hotspur Football Academy, multiple golf courses, parks, and a bustling town center with a Main Street feel. The district was also diverse in culture, income, and nationality. People from all over the world called it home, be they Greeks, Cypriots, Kurds, Nigerians, Ghanaians, Somalis, Afro-Caribbeans, or Bangladeshis. When those immigrant communities felt that they didn't belong, Joan made it her duty to help.

The district also had its problems. The east side of the A10 highway had a childhood poverty rate higher than both the UK and London average. Police budget cuts in 2010 contributed to Enfield becoming the worst area for serious youth violence in London. She worked closely with the local police borough commander and the chief superintendent to discuss possible steps to reverse the alarming trend and have more police deployed to increase public safety. Meanwhile, cuts to the health sector led to the closing of medical practices.

Through it all, Joan continued to fight for her constituents, believing that her party should be the vanguard of democracy, fairness, and equality. She hosted "coffee mornings" once a month on Saturday in a local school or community room with adequate parking; they would invite a couple thousand households in the area and typically get about seventy-five hardworking, everyday people to attend. Joan would also invite community leaders, members of the police department, and youth organizations to talk about the various issues that were important to the people. On some Sunday mornings, she and members of the party would go door-knocking in order to better understand the concerns of the constituents. In addition to speaking out about government budget cuts to healthcare and policing, she also addressed their concerns about education and housing. There was a shortage of quality housing, and rental prices were increasing, all of which had changed the landscape of what was once a reasonably priced borough. Very few MPs went to such great lengths to meet with the people and hear what they had to say. It was because of those efforts that she learned the needs of the community firsthand.

She was liked and respected by her constituents and her colleagues, but that started to change in 2015 when she was asked to become the chair of Labour Friends of Israel (LFI), an organization dedicated to strengthening the relationship between the United Kingdom and Israel. They support a two-state solution to the Israeli–Palestinian conflict and worked closely with the Israeli Labor Party to reduce violence and spread democracy.

Joan felt that the LFI represented the mainstream views of the party. Former Labour Party leaders Harold Wilson, Jim Callaghan, Tony Blair, and Gordon Brown honored the principles the party was founded on by standing up to racism, but the party started to transform when Jeremy Corbyn took control that year. The Labour Party now had a leader who called Hamas and Hezbollah – both of which have been declared terrorist organizations by the United States and consider themselves at war with Israel – his "friends." He had personal links to Holocaust deniers and antisemites. He refused to deny that the existence of Israel is a racist endeavor, choosing instead to side with the ayatollah of Iran, a brutal regime with a history of human rights atrocities and the sworn mortal enemy of Israel.

Corbyn and the Labour Party seemed to be echoing far-fetched conspiracies founded on antisemitic tropes that involved the Rothschilds, Zionists, and the "Israel lobby's" power – all disproven theories that powerful Jewish leaders are attempting to control the world by manipulating various institutions like the stock market, legal system, and education. Despite the best efforts of Joan and other members, the party that was once an ally of the British Jewish community and the Israeli Labor Party had been taken over by the far left and was in the process of alienating the only democracy in the Middle East.

Joan's support of Israel soon made her a target within her own party. She was attacked from inside and out. An undercover reporter from Al Jazeera tried to tarnish her reputation during the September 2016 Labour Party Conference by filming her confronting an antisemitic incident, but it didn't deter her. In July 2017, she rallied colleagues to get the UK to appropriate £3 million for Israeli–Palestinian people-to-people exchanges, an initiative five years in the making. Ever committed to compromise, she felt it was imperative that her own government reach across the aisle to build bridges; if they couldn't work with those who had different views to find a way forward, how could they possibly tell the Israelis and Palestinians that they had to work together?

The March of the Living

The International March of the Living was created in 1988, and the three-kilometer walk from Auschwitz to Birkenau in Poland is held every year on Holocaust Remembrance Day as a tribute to the six million Jews who were murdered. The march also serves as a counterpoint to Nazi death marches, during which the Third Reich forced at least a quarter of a million victims to traverse great distances under horrific conditions between the summer of 1944 right up until the Nazi surrender in May 1945. The death rate during these marches was often 50 percent.

April 25, 2018, was the thirtieth anniversary of the March of the Living, and it happened to coincide with Israel's seventieth birthday. Israeli president Reuven Rivlin and Polish president Andrzej Duda joined the thousands of participants from all faiths, backgrounds, and countries. Diverse delegations came from every continent, from Australia to Argentina.

Joan quickly volunteered to join the delegation from the United Kingdom. It wouldn't be her first trip to Poland; she had previously accompanied other MPs and student leaders as part of the London-based nonprofit the Holocaust Educational Trust. They visited Auschwitz and participated in a prayer service at Birkenau. Seminars focused on how to identify and combat antisemitism, and students were given the chance to speak with survivors. Joan said the program was immensely powerful, and she continued to mentor students afterwards on numerous issues, including confronting the BDS (Boycott, Divestment and Sanctions) campaign and dealing with antisemitism on university campuses.

The 2018 trip had special significance and came at a crucial time for Joan. Prior commitments forced her to catch up with the British delegation, comprising hundreds of students and community leaders, three days after their arrival in Krakow. Before her flight, she read remarkable survival stories that reminded her of the work she had done for the museum thirty years earlier. It was by sheer coincidence that shortly after her arrival, she met the sister of Freddie Knoller, the Holocaust survivor whose profile she had read back in 1986 and who inspired her to tell the stories of survivors. It was her introduction to "Jewish geography," as people from all over the world were comparing notes with strangers and finding friends and family they had in common.

After spending the night at a youth hostel, the delegation boarded three buses in the morning bound for Auschwitz. The attendees were in their thousands and from all over the globe, yet many were draped in the Israeli flag, and there was a universal language of mutual respect and optimism. The march wasn't only a chance to mourn the devastating loss of life seven decades earlier; it was also a celebration of those who survived the horrors of the Holocaust. Simultaneously, it was a way to celebrate Israel's anniversary and all that had been accomplished during the previous decades. Emotions were high, and Joan was elated that she could duck away from London for these few days and have the honor to participate.

A tour followed the march, which took the delegation to Belzec and then on to Majdanek, where they met with the other buses for a prayer session. They stopped at the village of Zbylitowska Góra outside of Tarnow, which looked like the kind of place you would go to for a picnic but was in reality a mass grave where eight hundred children were massacred after the Nazis took over the area on September 7, 1939.

During the tour, Joan received a call from the Israeli Labor Party chairman and well-known politician Isaac Herzog. Joan knew him well enough and thought about the unique coincidence that he was calling at this very moment, when she was with so many shared allies and friends. She picked up the phone and called him by his nickname, Bougie, but he did not have time for pleasantries or chit chat. He explained that the Israeli Labor Party would be formally breaking relations with the Labour Party due to his counterpart, Jeremy Corbyn. She felt such mixed emotions. She knew that she needed to prepare a press statement, but she also felt it was disrespectful to even think of a matter like that in such a solemn location.

On the two-hour flight home, she wondered how the Polish locals could live so close to the camps back in the 1940s, yet still manage to look the other way. The thought was haunting and depressing. She didn't want to compare the 1940s with their current situation, but it made her think. How could she expect to tell ordinary citizens to stand up and speak out against injustice if she didn't with fellow MPs and members of her own party? It was unacceptable for elected officials to utter antisemitic statements or look the other way when their peers did. She was reminded of the famous quote popularized by Elie Wiesel: "The opposite of love is not hate, it's indifference."

No Confidence

Labour had become a party within a party, and leadership no longer recognized Joan as one of their own. The Corbyn regime had taken control of all the senior positions in every region, so it wasn't much of a surprise when, on September 6, 2018, the local party staged a no-confidence vote. When Joan did some digging, she quickly learned that the meeting was a well-orchestrated set up that had been planned for three months.

The vote itself was a show trial, and the result had no lasting meaning. She would remain in office no matter what the outcome, but a vote of no confidence in Joan would be a huge PR win for the Labour Party. Never one to back down from a fight, she felt that she had no choice but to attend; she couldn't let people think they could push her around in her own constituency. Joan convinced ten friends to help her spend the evening phoning key party allies, asking that they take time to attend the vote. There were a thousand members in the area, and most of them had never attended a single party meeting.

The meeting was held in a small hall owned by the local Labour Party and was set to begin at 8 p.m., but it was delayed because the membership secretary couldn't keep up with how many people were checking in at the door. It was packed full of constituents who rarely came to meetings and only attended this one because they had been recruited by one of the two sides. Some attendees didn't have enough time to arrange for babysitters, so they brought their young children. Many new faces were teenagers, as you can become a party member at the age of fourteen. It was chaos, and they were dangerously close to being in breach of the fire code.

The overwhelmed twenty-one-year-old local party chair officially started his very first meeting at 8:30 p.m. and, right from the outset, he struggled to keep order as the atmosphere turned nasty. During the proceeding, the chairman tried to warn against recording and reminded everyone that it was a private meeting, so no press was allowed. It wasn't until later that they realized that the event had been live-streamed on the Iranian state-controlled news, PressTV.

Joan sat patiently in the third row with her closest friends. She was only allowed to speak for three minutes before the vote was called. It was so crowded and there was so much disorder that it took forty-five minutes to hand out the ballot papers and count the votes. A group of Joan's supporters had to leave because it was taking so long.

Before the vote was announced, Joan learned that she had lost. It was close, but she ultimately fell short, 94 votes to 92. She didn't want to give her opponents the satisfaction of seeing her reaction when the result was revealed, so she decided to leave. Outside the hall, she was consoled by her most stalwart supporters, some of whom were crying. The vote stung, but she assured everyone that she would not be stepping down.

Once back home, Joan poured a glass of wine and, against her better judgment and her husband's advice, sent out a tweet blaming her defeat on the "Trots Stalinists Communists [sic] and assorted hard left." The next morning, Joan canceled a school visit because she knew the media would be there, which would be unfair to the kids. Instead, she spoke to the press in the afternoon and attacked fellow MP and party head Jeremy Corbyn for his bullying and abuse. Jeremy Corbyn was trying to build uniformity, and Joan realized that publicly airing the party's division was more important than actual victory over the Conservatives.

Former prime minister Tony Blair sent Joan a text message telling her to be brave, and Joan spent the weekend trying to celebrate her birthday, but a grey cloud hung in the air, and she wasn't in the mood to celebrate.

Later that month, Blair told the BBC that it was a different type of party under Jeremy Corbyn, adding that many felt the party was lost and couldn't be regained.

Things Get Worse before They Get Better

With the rise of ISIS, the United Kingdom experienced an uptick in attacks on British soil, with two of the most prominent being the Westminster terrorist attacks of 2017 and 2018. Despite their political differences, everyone working in Parliament was suddenly united when the MPs were ushered into the House of Commons Chambers and the doors were locked by counterterrorism police dressed in full riot gear and carrying automatic weapons. While the police searched the building, groups huddled together, regardless of party, and did so for hours in the countless nooks and crannies of the old Parliament building.

That memorable experience was a striking reminder for Joan of how vile the bitter political rivalries had gotten. When she was a teacher, she told her students to never give in to bullies, and she thought Jeremy Corbyn was a bully. Joan was among a group of MPs who felt that he was not fit to lead; he had so many opportunities to do something about the growing antisemitism in the party, but neither he nor his supporters chose to do anything about it.

She felt that his hatred of Israel led to a hatred of Jews and allowed British Jews to be abused with impunity. Those who attempted to stand up to what they saw as unjust were singled out, attacked, and bullied into silence. She never claimed to know what Jeremy Corbyn truly felt in his heart, but she knew that actions spoke louder than words. There was no indication that anything would change, so she had no choice but to leave the party in February 2019. Once she tweeted out her resignation letter, she felt relief. She could finally focus on what she was supposed to be doing as MP and address kitchen-table issues facing the British people in the tumult leading up to Brexit.

Joan knew there would be fallout and that resigning from the party was only the beginning. The personal attacks continued, and in early 2019, the death threats began. An anonymous letter called her a "Jew whore," who should be "shoved back in the ovens." Dead rats were left on the doorstep of her home on two separate occasions. One morning, a photocopied note with cutout letters was left on her desk in Parliament, which meant that someone with a Parliament ID had gained access to her office overnight. On another occasion, someone taped a picture of a train, in reference to the Holocaust, on her office door. Joan told me that the constituents became uncomfortable with visiting her local office in Enfield, as did the diligent staff, who had panic buttons under their desks. The threats had gotten so extreme that the police installed covert surveillance, and a car with blacked-out windows and two security personnel sat outside her constituency office. Luckily, personal protection was not new for her. Never once did she consider changing course or stopping her vocal support for what she believed to be the basic principles of inclusion and equality. The threats only strengthened her resolve to stand up against both the far left and far right whenever they attacked.

A New Beginning

The lights were blinding when Joan took the stage at the Washington Convention Center on March 24, 2019, to speak to the crowd of over eighteen thousand gathered at the annual American Israel Public Affairs Committee (AIPAC) Policy Conference. Except for a rally in Trafalgar Square, she had never spoken to such a large crowd, and this was certainly the largest group she had ever spoken to indoors. She remained calm as she read her speech off the teleprompter. She talked about the importance of standing one's ground when condemning antisemitism and warned everyone to stay on guard because things could change quickly, as she had witnessed in her own party. She stressed the importance of calling out politicians on both sides of the aisle who questioned Israel's right to exist.

The speech was met with resounding applause. After everything she had been through, she appreciated the approval from such a diverse audience. She wanted to stay and soak in the atmosphere but had to catch a flight, so she hustled her way through the hordes of people backstage who wanted to take her picture. Thirty minutes later, she was out the door and on the way to the airport, still running on adrenaline. For the first time, it occurred to her how her seemingly small decision to leave the Labour Party had resonated widely across the Atlantic.

Joan retained her position as chair of the Labour Friends of Israel and was named honorary president in August 2019, but knew that it was time to begin a new chapter. The following month, she announced that she would not be running for office again. She continued to be an outspoken critic of politicians who peddled hate and antisemitic tropes. She publicly stated that she would not be voting for Jeremy Corbyn in the December 12, 2019, general election. Joan's support for relations with Israel in Parliament defined her legacy.

On election night, Joan spent the night at home, packing for her trip to Israel the following morning. The car was coming to pick her up at 8 a.m., but she still couldn't sleep, so she stayed up late into the night and watched as Jeremy Corbyn and the Labour Party suffered a historic landslide defeat.

CHAPTER 7

Chloé Valdary
Daringly Enigmatic

When her high school was giving away books, fifteen-year-old Chloé Valdary was drawn to *Mila 18* by Leon Uris. She didn't know of the author or the subject matter. She judged a book by its cover, literally, and it changed her life.

Once she started reading, she was drawn in by the tale of the Nazi occupation of Poland during WWII and the atrocities committed against the Jewish people. It was unusual that a teenage girl from New Orleans would find herself fascinated with Eastern European Jewish culture and heritage, but Chloé's upbringing was anything but ordinary.

Born in Gentilly, New Orleans, in 1993, Chloé was one of five girls raised in a non-Jewish philosemitic home. Her father was Baptist but had converted to become a pre-Constantine Christian when Chloé was three, a doctrine that teaches that before Constantine became emperor of Rome over seventeen hundred years prior, he observed the Sabbath and kept the holy days. That's what Chloé's family did. They kept kosher, and Chloé even took the Jewish holidays off from school. On Fridays, they'd have Bible study, and on Saturday, they'd go to church. Even though Louisiana was an overwhelmingly Christian state, the family didn't celebrate Christmas or participate in the annual Easter parade. Instead, they put a unique spin on studying the Scripture. Their tradition on these days was to read Roman Catholic church doctrine; it was a more intellectual exercise than the typical cultural practice of exchanging gifts or hunting for Easter eggs.

The more Chloé learned about the origins of Christianity, the more she realized how much of a world existed outside New Orleans.

The city of New Orleans has always been a melting pot, with distinct influences from the Spanish and French empires as well as African slaves and Chitimacha and Choctaw tribes. Because of its unique history, the city was one of the first in the country to not only value education for women but also to emphasize the need for the creative arts. While attending Langston Hughes Elementary, she learned a lot about Black history in a way that was rooted in empowerment and told through a narrative of redemption. Literary pillars of Black America loomed large in her imagination as she became steeped in the writings of Langston Hughes, Maya Angelou, and other poets and writers from the previous century.

When Chloé entered the magnet charter high school, she found herself among a much more culturally and racially diverse student body and quickly became friends with kids from all different backgrounds. Benjamin Franklin High School happened to be located on Leon C. Simon Drive – a street named after a prominent Jewish New Orleanian who was the branch director of the Atlanta Federal Reserve Bank during the Great Depression and widely credited with advancing Louisiana's unique economic concerns.

As she got older, Chloé continued to devour Jewish literature – a love she shared with her father, with whom she had many in-depth discussions on the topic. She was a member of the Hebrew Culture Club and was able to hone her writing and public speaking skills. She felt that literature and writing were in her blood and continued to be drawn in by the rich Jewish culture. She read *Exodus* and every other book by Leon Uris. She recognized her own story in the James Wheldon Johnson song "Lift Every Voice and Sing." She identified with the kids in the movie *Freedom Writers* (2007) who learned to choose love over hate after learning the story of Anne Frank.

With a burgeoning interest in screenwriting developing prior to graduation, Chloé was accepted at the University of New Orleans in 2011 as a film major, but she would continue to be drawn to her first love and cultural upbringing.

A New Spin on an Old Tradition

In 2011, two young terrorists brutally murdered five members of a Jewish family in Israel. The following year, a twenty-three-year-old terrorist went on a killing spree in Toulouse, France, that left seven dead and five wounded, some of whom were children and teachers at a Jewish school. The killers were close to Chloé in age. That made an impact and reinforced that this would be a fight for her generation.

Those tragedies were part of an overall increase in antisemitism in Europe, and 2011 was a new height for BDS activism on United States college campuses. The movement encourages boycotts of Israeli institutions and companies, dissuades banks and other institutions from investing in Israel, and pressures governments to end all business and trade with Israel.

Chloé is not Jewish, but given her upbringing, she took antisemitism personally and felt that the pro-Israel community was not effective enough in combatting it. She found that many students on campus didn't truly understand what Zionism was all about. To her, Zionism wasn't about the Jewish people having a place of refuge; it was a love story between a people and their land, traditions, and culture. It was about a people's capacity to love, even when that love was not reciprocated. One hundred years earlier, Zionism was a response to Jewish passivity, and it was once again time for the people to be proactive. All the while, she kept reading and learning. Elie Wiesel's harrowing tale of a concentration camp survivor in *The Town beyond the Wall* solidified her belief that what made us fundamentally human was the ability to engage in the act of choice. We can choose to be good and we can choose to be evil, but first we must choose. It was fundamentally inhuman to be indifferent.

Chloé's eyes were being opened, and she wasn't on campus long before she felt compelled to change her major from film to international studies. More significantly, she grew inspired to combat BDS and the misrepresentations about Israel by starting her own pro-Israel student organization. Nobody was telling the Jewish story, so she decided to step up to fill that void. But as with everything she did, she came at the topic from a completely original angle.

Nearby Tulane University also had a pro-Israel organization on campus that Chloé collaborated with. Even though it was also located in New Orleans, it might as well have been on a different planet. The student body was significantly more racially, religiously, and geographically diverse, and it had one of the largest percentages of Jewish students of any private college in the country. Chloé knew that she would never be able to convince antisemites on American college campuses to change their ideology, so she set out to appeal to the vast majority of students who either didn't know anything about Israel or did not care, in an attempt to educate them.

She and her organization began working closely with fellow student leaders at Tulane to organize a music festival called Declare Your Freedom. There were tents and outdoor exhibits that showed how Zionism connected to other prominent cultural movements, like the civil rights and indigenous peoples' movements. They hosted speakers, most of whom were non-Jews. A few protestors made an appearance but were mostly ignored, and that's when Chloé learned one of the most valuable lessons in the fight against antisemitism: people instinctively choose celebration over negativity. The goal was to give people permission to celebrate Zionism and help them associate Zionism with an awesome festival experience. Instead of trying to destroy something terrible on campus, she set out to create something spectacular and emotional in its place, thus making the BDS movement seem irrelevant. Over time, they were slowly able to make an impact and change the culture at both UNO and Tulane.

Activism brought Chloé into the world of public speaking, and it was a role she had been unknowingly prepared for since childhood. As a sophomore, her speeches about Israel and growing antisemitism made enough of an impact that she got selected to join a group of campus leaders for an intense professional development trip to Israel.

Many Jews, upon setting foot in Israel for the first time, describe a feeling that resembles returning home. What Chloé experienced was different: it was the feeling of arriving in the epicenter of humanity. She couldn't help but be reminded of the powerful and unique sense that Israel shaped civilization. During their stay, the students engaged in sightseeing and participated in a program with local host families called Shabbat of a Lifetime, during which some of the students even sang songs with their host families and taught them about American music.

Not only were all of the students non-Jewish, but they were divided almost evenly politically when it came to their views on the Israeli–Palestinian conflict. Despite their differences, there was love between the two groups, and even if many of their political opinions were unchanged after the trip, they were all able to see the human being in those they disagreed with.

Life on the Road

The coveted Tikvah Summer Fellowship is given to young leaders inspired by Jewish civilization, so they can study the political and cultural questions facing modern Jews while working on independent projects intended to strengthen the Jewish community. Upon graduation in 2015, Chloé became a recipient. She moved to New York City to begin working at the *Wall Street Journal* and was given the opportunity to be mentored by columnist Bret Stephens. She was assigned to write a paper and wanted to write about the psychology of connection and why people gravitate toward certain things. Stephens challenged her to learn what all of the Fortune 500 marketing campaigns had in common and use the newspaper's vast resources to study up on pop culture.

As a Nike fanatic who loved everything associated with the popular brand, she took a closer look at how the company operated. Branding soon became an obsession, and she studied another pop culture phenom in Beyoncé. That's when she realized the common denominator for successful brands: they don't market the product, they sell inspiration. Whether it was Nike or Beyoncé, they created content that reflected their *audience's* potential. She thought: What if the same concept that makes people gravitate toward certain brands could also be used to heal disconnection in other areas? That was an aha moment, and she couldn't help but see a parallel between what she'd learned and the way she had been trying to speak about Israel – not as a culture steeped in victimhood, but one that comes from a place of pride in identity and confidence about what its people can bring to the table of civilization.

She was beginning to develop a complex worldview, but it was during a vacation to Rome with a Jewish friend that same year that a significant piece of the puzzle fell into place and provided her with the inspiration needed to change her life. As soon as the plane touched down in Rome, she was transported back in time. The beautiful city shaped not only world history but also her own upbringing.

After a brief stop in Poland so her travel companion could attend the March of the Living, Chloé was back on a plane for a long flight home. Still wrestling with her recent ideas, she tried to relax and find perspective in Ethan Dor-Shav's philosophical take on Ecclesiastes. Far from light reading, the text explores King Solomon's confrontation with his own mortality. She knew she was on the cusp of something great, but it wasn't until she returned home and spoke with her mentor Bret Stephens about her experience that everything started to click. He used the word *enchantment*, and suddenly, everything came full circle, and she realized how to combine her two passions: Israel and pop culture.

Right then, Chloé committed to keeping the legacy of the past alive while finding a way to make it appealing to the millennial generation. Up to that point, she had found the conversation and argument within the pro-Israel community to be too neurotic and myopic, because it was rooted in fear and crisis. That conversation frequently touched upon the same grievances, but no matter how justified those grievances were, they didn't compel her generation to care deeply or to take action. She knew that to strike that chord, they needed to frame the conversation in a way that made it resonate with the new audience by appealing to their perspective and values. How do you appeal to millennials? You make the subject matter more fashionable, artistic, and emotionally compelling. Given her obsession with pop culture and branding, she felt that there was no better person to shift the conversation and deliver that message.

The next piece of the puzzle fell into place when Chloé landed her dream job in the fall of 2016 at Jerusalem U, where she got paid to produce pro-Israel social media content and speak to audiences worldwide. Following in the footsteps of fellow advocates Pastor Dumisani Washington of Christians United for Israel and Brooke Goldstein of the Lawfare Project, she set out to educate young Jews and activists who weren't yet educated about Zionism or Israel by framing her message as it had never been done before. She wanted to zoom out of the stale, circular debate and transcend the divisive politics by talking about the bigger picture. That didn't mean avoiding the obvious conflicts surrounding Israel, but rather framing the discussion differently – focusing on statehood, family, and ritual.

To Chloé, Zionism was about self-actualization and people realizing their innate dignity. They established a nation and rebuilt their homeland. It's easy to forget that when living in such an interconnected world, but people in every country around the world have something unique to say, and Jews are no exception. There is dignity in difference, and Chloé wanted to remind everyone of the potential in all human beings. Israel has thrived because of people who have gone beyond their own limitations to accomplish the impossible, and when you aspire to great things, your dreams can become a vision for your future.

While crisscrossing the globe, Chloé's travel schedule was a blur. In Aspen, she found herself in the summer playground for incredibly high net-worth Jews who were hanging on her every word. In Berlin, she joined the German consul general to Israel to engage with millennials from diverse backgrounds. She found that the students at the forefront of the pro-Israel movement in Germany were left-wing, the opposite of what it was typically like in the United States. In Los Angeles, she found herself in an Orthodox synagogue on Pico Boulevard talking about Kendrick Lamar and dissecting his song "DNA." She felt that the lyrics captured the human condition and the ability to both build up and destroy.

Chloé often evoked pop culture and history during her speeches. She explained how Martin Luther King used language from the Bible and how the Dalai Lama, Bob Marley, Salvador Dalí, and Nina Simone all drew inspiration from the Zionist movement. And if it inspired them, it could undoubtedly inspire another generation. She wanted to carry on that legacy by making her talks an experience; she wanted the audience to have fun and to feel alive just like when listening to good music. She wanted to give them something they would never forget.

The two years following the 2016 presidential election in the United States were a period of heightened activism and political awareness. Chloé found herself engaged in some heated debates, including a 2018 panel discussion on cultural boycotts of Israel hosted by author, professor, and activist for the Palestinian cause Marc Lamont Hill. Chloé described it as an atmosphere of palpable antisemitism and hatred toward Israel. Despite being outnumbered, she not only shined but was beginning to bring a certain sophistication to the Israeli–Palestinian debate that she felt had been absent in many of the discussions she had participated in. By that point, Chloé had learned that antisemitism, or any form of racism, had little to do with the people being discriminated against and more to do with the offenders overcompensating for feelings of self-hatred and a lack of security, both material and existential. The contempt of another was driven by an attempt to control or make sense of a chaotic life. That revelation allowed her to take a different approach.

As each side of the Israeli–Palestinian debate dug their heels in, the campus discussions and public forums often turned into shouting matches. Each side assumed the negative motives and bad faith of the other. Chloé observed what was *not* happening during those discussions, and instead of striving to be the louder and angrier voice in the room, started to approach discussions and debates from a place of love, respect, and compassion. The goal was to educate and influence, not provide red meat to those who were already on her side, which was the approach so many pundits and talking heads took when arguing the issues. A realization was forming along with an inspiration to go bigger and do more.

The Theory of Enchantment

Chloé's speeches attracted attention, and she soon realized that there was an audience for what she had to say, but something didn't sit right, despite her success. She found professional activism antithetical to her values because to earn a living combatting antisemitism, antisemitism needed to exist in the first place. There had to be a better way. She had always known that she wanted to be her own boss eventually, so she began to plan out the next phase of her life.

Enchantment was the word Bret Stephens used when describing Chloé's experience in Rome. That concept, along with the lessons learned when crafting her paper about the psychology of connection, became the foundation for her Theory of Enchantment. This wasn't a new endeavor as much as it was the evolution of the principles she had been lecturing about for years. Chloé wanted to combat the negative conversations that circulated around a range of topics. She believed that to change the conversation, you had to change the framework. In the context of intersectionality or anti-Israel sentiment, that framework was based on assumptions about the other. Chloé refined the concepts in her speech until she boiled it down to three principles that she drew upon when engaged in heated political discussions:

1. Treat people like human beings, not political abstractions.
2. Criticize to uplift and empower, never to tear down, never to destroy.
3. Root everything you do in love and compassion.

Her philosophy evolved into an educational course that utilized social-emotional learning, and, just like the essence of her speeches, was taught through pop culture. It was based on the idea that one could build character and develop virtue based on those three principles. Inspired to move on to the next phase of her life, she put traveling and speaking on hold to launch her business, an antiracism program called Theory of Enchantment.

After spending three months developing her course, Chloé began reaching out to every university in America, but heard back from none. She expanded her search to include homeschooling parents, nonprofit leaders, school districts, and corporate leaders. Then, just when she began to build momentum, the world came to a screeching halt.

Working from home in Brooklyn, Chloé found herself in the epicenter of the COVID-19 outbreak. It would have been easy to quit, and she had every opportunity to put the operation on hold, but she continued to grow her business during the global pandemic. Something bigger was happening. A few months earlier, on New Year's Eve, she told a friend that 2020 would be the best year ever; her friend said it would be the worst. Pandemic aside, Chloé was committed to the same principles of healing disconnection that she outlined when at the *Wall Street Journal*. She believed that crisis required an examination of your moral compass and ethical grounding. COVID-19 may have thrust the world into chaos, but it didn't slow her down or prevent her from charging forward.

She knew that people would be terrified due to experiencing cognitive dissonance. The way we thought the world worked was being thrust upside down. Everyone experienced chaos in some form or another, and the people who eventually rose to the top were the ones who could take that chaos and turn it into order and meaning. That required reexamining what we stand for and grounding ourselves in a moral ethic, which is precisely what the Theory of Enchantment was all about and why her business continued to grow.

Travel was severely limited, and she wasn't able to give any speeches for a long time, but Chloé rode out the chaos by meditating for an hour every day and returning to a practice that had been a natural outlet since she was young: writing. She continued to pen op-eds for publications such as *USA Today*.

It wasn't long before her persistence paid off, and Chloé found herself on the map when she received an offer to train the Office of Civil Rights at the Federal Aviation Administration. That contract provided her the social capital to expand her business, and she went on to receive calls from other clinics, nonprofits, and assorted organizations geared toward educating kids.

Chloé Valdary has yet to turn thirty, and she has already become a powerful social entrepreneur and digital influencer who has inspired community leaders three times her age. Her identity was shaped at the intersection of two faiths that are too often at odds: Christianity and Judaism. She has dedicated a large portion of her life to Israel. Every time she set foot in the country, she felt that special enchantment in the air that was unlike anywhere else on earth. The great story of the Jewish people continues to inspire her while reinforcing her belief in the human experience and that people have the potential to overcome tremendous odds. Anything is possible.

CHAPTER 8
Father Patrick Desbois
Patiently Truthful

There is no murder without witnesses.

That was the message Father Patrick Desbois took from the story in the Bible that has resonated with him the most throughout the years: Cain and Abel. When Cain, a farmer and the firstborn son of Adam and Eve, murdered his shepherd brother, Abel, out of jealousy, Cain's crime did not go unpunished. He was banished. That message has become Father Patrick's primary motivation and the engine that has driven him to document the atrocities of the Holocaust. Now a devout French Roman Catholic priest, he didn't find religion until adulthood.

Born ten years after the end of WWII, Patrick was raised in Bordeaux hearing stories about the war that had unfolded in his own backyard. One stood out. It was the most vague and mysterious of them all. It took place in a town far away with a funny-sounding name: Rava-Ruska. The story involved his grandfather, Claudis, a former French soldier sent to a prisoner of war camp in Ukraine. A fun-loving and comical guy most of the time, his grandfather would not discuss the camp, and nobody in the family knew what had happened to him there. Patrick assumed the worst and worried that his grandfather might have killed people.

After much persistence, Claudis slowly began to open up about life in the camp – the lack of food and water and even his escape attempts. The picture he painted was bleak, but one phrase stood out to Patrick: "It was much worse for the people on the outside." He was perplexed and asked himself, *What could possibly be worse than this camp?* That first conversation at the age of seven piqued his interest, but it wasn't until a trip to the library in Chalon-sur-Saône five years later that he put the pieces together. He learned that the tragedy his grandfather witnessed involved the fate of the Jewish people. That realization began what would become a lifelong mission to study the Jewish religion and culture and to learn the truth about what happened during the Holocaust.

Patrick was ordained in 1986 at the age of thirty-one. While he was the superior of the Grand Seminary in Prado, Lyon, in 1992, he also served as the secretary of Jewish relations for three prominent cardinals. In 1999, he was appointed secretary to the French Conference of Bishops for Relations with the Jewish community. Still, he could never shake the feeling that God was calling on him to do something specific.

The First Step

Father Patrick was young when he heard his grandfather speak about the camp for the last time, but when he traveled to Ukraine in 2002 for the first time, it felt like he had been there before. When asked at the border if it was his first trip, he told the guard that he had been there "a long time ago."

Father Patrick was traveling to Poland as part of an apostolic voyage to dedicate the new basilica at the Divine Mercy Sanctuary in Kraków. This church had been designated a shrine in 1968, for it housed the remains of Sister Faustina. He didn't set out to see the camp where his grandfather had been imprisoned during the war but, by chance, his travels took him nearby. After a sleepless night, he made a point to visit the small Ukrainian village of Rava-Ruska, located on the border of Poland. He knew from the archives that eighteen thousand Jews and twenty-five thousand Soviet prisoners had been killed there, but the local mayor claimed to have no idea where it happened or what happened to the bodies because, he said, they were all killed in secret. It was a small village, so Father Patrick found it unlikely that over forty thousand people could be murdered without anyone knowing. Ukraine had only declared itself an independent country a decade earlier, but its residents maintained their Soviet mentality and were disinclined to openly discuss their dark past with outsiders, if at all. But Father Patrick would not take no for an answer.

It took three more trips to Rava-Ruska before he finally got the answers he sought, and they came from a new mayor who was much less Soviet-minded and more eager to reveal the truth. "People are waiting for you," the mayor said before escorting Father Patrick into a waiting limo that took them even further off the beaten path to a small hamlet, where they met with fifty elderly villagers and farmers. Together, the group walked into the nearby forest and revealed the mass gravesite where the last of the fifteen hundred Jews of Rava-Ruska were buried. The villagers were all children at the time of the genocide, and many had never discussed the events with another living soul, but they all had something to say and told their stories with vivid clarity.

The horror began the night a Nazi soldier arrived in the village on a motorcycle and then quickly left before daybreak. The locals wondered what he was doing. Little did they know that he was the architect; it was his job to calculate the volume of the grave by tallying up the number of Jews in the village. The next day, Nazi soldiers returned with thirty Jews and forced them to dig the mass grave. The soldiers made the children run errands and guard the Jews. They forced the older teenagers to help with the digging. When the soldiers got bored, they tracked down a gramophone to listen to German music. One of the soldiers played a harmonica but discarded it when it broke (this harmonica was later found with a metal detector when Father Patrick and the villagers returned to further examine the site). The soldiers then ordered the Jews out of the grave while a Ukrainian policeman secretly put an explosive in the pit. When the Jews returned to dig, the bomb was detonated, and all thirty Jews were killed.

One of the elderly women recalled how the Nazi soldiers forced her to climb up into the nearby trees to remove pieces of the corpses that had scattered during the explosion. She was to hide them back in the mass grave before the next truckload of Jews arrived. That went on for an entire day. When new Jews arrived, they were all lined up at the top of the pit before they were executed. The soldiers designated just one bullet for one Jew, so many of them didn't die from the gunshot and were buried alive. Once the last Jew was shot, the grave was covered, and the Germans left, but blood continued to bubble up from the dirt. For three days, witnesses recall seeing the ground move; that was how long it took for some of the victims to die.

Given the vivid detail each witness added, it felt as if the incident had occurred only a month before. Everything from the weather to the conversations that were had and even the expressions on some of the soldiers' faces made this horrific crime feel so real. Father Patrick had educated himself on the horrors of the Holocaust, but to be in the spot where the killings took place and hear witnesses explain how it happened accentuated the horror of the situation in a way that was almost too much for him to handle. He knew why his grandfather never wanted to share what he had witnessed. So many questions raced through his mind. *How could so few kill so many? How had this story not been told before? How had this remained a secret for so long?* He wasn't prepared for what he learned that day. It could have ended there, but before he left Ukraine, the mayor told him, "What I did for you in this one village, I can do for you in a hundred villages."

Father Patrick can't explain why the mayor said that or why he agreed to help, but it would forever change his life. He left Ukraine knowing that what he needed to do next was much bigger than him. He would need his faith, and he would need a team.

A Group Effort

Cardinal Jean-Marie Lustiger, the archbishop in Paris from 1981 to 2005, was the first person Father Patrick spoke with upon his return. The cardinal was born to a Polish-Jewish family in Bedzin and lost his mother in Auschwitz. His later conversion to Christianity was considered controversial by some. Father Patrick served as an aide for the cardinal and also looked to him as a mentor who attempted to bridge the gap between Catholicism and Judaism. This proved to be another opportunity, and in 2004, they created the non-profit organization Yahad-In Unum. The name (which means "Together" in Hebrew and in Latin) embodied the mission: in Hebrew and in Latin, the organization would aim to bring people together.

The team consisted of twenty-nine other people from all over the world who were a mix of Catholic, Protestant, Eastern Orthodox, and non-believers. Twenty-five were based in Paris, with two working at the archives in Germany and two working at the archives in Russia. Their mission was to collect information about the mass killing of Jews in Eastern Europe and the former Soviet Union between 1941 and 1945. The Eastern Front was one of the deadliest arenas of the war. These brutal and bloody battles, many fought during relentless winter conditions, accounted for thirty million of the eighty-five million lives lost during the war. Cities and towns were devastated while the people starved and struggled to combat disease. All of that inhumane brutality had been made public knowledge, yet some of the worst atrocities still remained a secret. Father Patrick made it his life's work to find those killing fields. He knew that you could not build modern Europe on top of mass graves, for God would say the blood of Abel is crying out. For him, civilized humanity began with burying the dead, so that's what he set out to do.

The organization started their search by combing the archives and comparing the Soviet version of events with the German version and the survivor version, which often differed drastically. They used the data to build a map of the mass graves and chart the extermination, which unfolded across the length of an entire continent. It didn't matter if he was looking for a mass grave with forty thousand people or a family of four, he put the same amount of time into each endeavor because he knew how he would feel if his family were out there. The number of victims they discovered was far less important than giving meaning to their lost lives.

The final piece of the puzzle needed to pinpoint the locations was living witnesses. Much to the surprise of Father Desbois' investigative team, these mass killings were not done in private. It was legal to kill a Jew or Roma if you could prove it was for racial reasons, so many of the mass shootings in these villages were made public. Everyone saw everything. The Jews were being condemned to death, so it was viewed by some as a legal affair rather than genocide. The Nazis were proud of what they were doing and often organized a spectacle. One witness recalled a soldier allowing his young son to kill Jews.

When it came to conducting witness interviews, Father Patrick and his team were trained to listen, not to judge. The goal was to learn what happened and find the killers responsible. The first hurdle investigators needed to overcome when dealing with the various witnesses was cultural. All of these crimes were committed in the former Soviet Union. Not only were the team dealing with different government and military structures when in different jurisdictions, but the atmosphere was also different in each place they visited. There was no private property at the time. The people didn't have a choice. They did what they were told; they knew they would be killed if they didn't. The Soviet mentality was very different from what the interviewers were used to. These were people who were not looking for forgiveness or admitting fault; they did what they felt they had to do at the time to survive.

None of the interviewers knew the level of involvement of the people they were speaking to. By their faces alone, they had no way of knowing if they were speaking to someone who saved Jews or killed Jews, so they took an approach similar to detectives and interviewed a potential killer the same way they would interview a savior. Many of the people they spoke with had never spoken about what they witnessed to another living soul. The interviewers came to believe that some of the witnesses were waiting for them to arrive because they were eager to unload the burden before they died. Other witnesses wondered why it had taken so long for someone to come around and start asking questions.

Father Patrick began every one of his interviews the same way, by asking, "Were you here during the war?" He made sure to raise positive questions and prevent any of the witnesses from feeling guilty. Over time, the group pieced together the method of those killers who carried out this mass execution effort.

The *Einsatzgruppen* were German death squads with one goal: to kill. Shooters, cooks, and drivers exchanged roles interchangeably as they traveled from village to village. The Nazis set out to eliminate every Jew, from the oldest grandmother to the youngest child. If Hitler had been victorious in WWII, there is a chance that not a single Jew would be alive today.

These death squads would typically arrive at night and, in concert with members of the local police who had not left to join the Red Army, surround the village so no Jews could escape. That night, many of the soldiers and officers would also rape Jewish women. The soldiers never slept in the town where they killed, so they rounded up the Jews before dawn. The Jews were told that they were being deported via train to Palestine, which often occurred in the Soviet Union, so it seemed to many like a better option than being killed. Those who complied gathered their belongings and lined up outside. Those who didn't and tried to hide were tracked down and killed.

The mass grave had typically been dug ahead of time and in a location close to the train station. Once the soldiers diverted the caravan of Jews, they knew they would be killed and discarded their belongings so that they wouldn't be taken by the Nazis. The Jews were then led to one of two types of mass graves. The first type was circular, like the one in Rava-Ruska, and the Jews lined up around the edge so they would fall in after being shot. The second type was long, and the Jews were forced to lie on top of the corpses. After the killing was over and the grave covered, the Nazis spearheaded a common local Soviet tradition by hosting an auction the next day to sell the looted belongings of the dead.

In some villages, a car with a megaphone would drive around and instruct everyone to attend. The witnesses were all young during the war; many had been let out of school to attend executions. When Father Patrick asked why, he heard the same explanation: "They believed it was interesting for the children to see." Some were even told, "Today we kill our enemies, and school will resume tomorrow."

One revelation that confused Father Patrick for years was why so many people were eager to watch. Of the forty-seven hundred witnesses interviewed, he recalls only one of those people saying that they didn't stay to watch the murders. It was like that in every country. Still, why were people attracted to the murderous public display? Did it mean they didn't care? Some went to acquire belongings of the victims. A portion of the spectators were Christians who viewed what they witnessed as a divine revenge. Some prayed during what they considered a religious spectacle. However, not everyone who watched was complicit. Father Patrick compared the morbid fascination to people slowing down when driving past the scene of an accident. When individuals knew they were safe, they were much more open to watching people die, because they were left feeling they were on the right side. It was much more deeply linked to the human condition than he realized.

As their search for mass graves continued, many of the sites they discovered were open fields that appeared calm and peaceful; others were farmland with corn and tomato plants growing above the grave. Very few of the locals had any idea that thousands of bodies lay buried underneath their community after a mass killing decades earlier. However, the closer they looked, the more evidence they discovered. They found shell cartridges, bullets, and even guns left behind by the killers at many of the sites. As they got deeper, they'd find jewelry and valuables belonging to the victims. When they reached the bodies, they saw skulls with bullet holes and others who had been buried alive and died with their mouths open. Mothers were buried clutching their children.

Some of the digs were stopped after reaching that first layer of skeletons because of religious regulations. Jewish tradition forbids moving the dead once they have been buried, so not all of the sites were excavated. In those cases, they marked the sites using GPS only, for fear that a tangible landmark would attract looters.

After eighty research trips over ten years, the Yahad-In Unum team were able to identify over seventeen hundred mass graves (twelve hundred in Ukraine alone). They determined that 2.3 million Jews, Romani, communists, and homosexuals were killed by the Nazis during this time. Compare this to the 1.1 million who died at Auschwitz. These killings throughout Eastern Europe and the Former Soviet Union were not a Nazi afterthought; they were an attempt at mass extermination. The camps only existed because the Germans couldn't murder Jews in large cities, so they needed to find a way to separate them from the public. One of the survivors told Father Patrick, "At least in Auschwitz, we could sleep at night."

In 2008, Father Patrick published an account of his work in the book *The Holocaust by Bullets: A Priest's Journey to Uncover the Truth behind the Murder of 1.5 Million Jews*; he even walked a CBS *60 Minutes* camera crew across some of the mass graves in an effort to bring light to the horrible atrocities at the center of his life's work. Had Father Patrick and his team not started their search, the public would never have known that many of these mass graves existed. The secret would have died with the witnesses.

Father Patrick treated genocide not as a historical incident, but as a crime. Every Jew was killed by a person – not by a machine or an ideology, but by a relatively young soldier from Germany or Austria. He felt it was crucial to expose the guilty and seek justice for the victims. Most importantly, Father Patrick was committed to making sure these atrocities would never be denied by future generations.

An Eye toward the Future

After spending a decade searching for mass graves and providing thousands of families and communities with answers, Father Patrick had gained a reputation as an expert in mass killing – both the execution of and psychology behind the morbid human phenomenon.

It was 2014, during a work trip to Guatemala, when he first learned of the attempt by ISIS to eradicate the Yazidi population in Sinjar, Iraq. Unlike his previous work, which involved investigating events that occurred over seventy years in the past, this was an example of ongoing genocide. He had been alive during the Rwandan genocide in 1994 and promised himself that he would not stand by again. He knew he had to go. After taking three days to pray, he traveled to Iraq.

Sinjar had been reduced to rubble. Even before the destruction, it was not a place for French Catholic priests. For the Kurdish forces to liberate the city, they had to destroy it, and there was very little left when Father Patrick began his investigation. The setting was different, as were the killers, but the mission in Iraq was the same for Yahad-In Unum as in Eastern Europe. They interviewed survivors and began to map out the prisons, torture sites, and mass graves. They searched for evidence of the crimes committed, listened to the witnesses, and used that information to find the murderers and help bring justice for the victims, because until there is justice, people will forget – or worse, deny the existence of the crime.

What Father Patrick discovered in Iraq surprised him. The eradication efforts of ISIS were more sophisticated than he had expected. They saw the Yazidi people as devil worshipers and set out to destroy them, and they had a plan for everyone. Some were brainwashed and trained to become soldiers, others sex slaves, while members of the population who didn't serve an immediate purpose were killed.

What ISIS and other more recent genocidal regimes have in common is that they did not want to create another Auschwitz. Many felt that the creation of concentration camps was a flaw in Hitler's grand plan, because the camps created a tangible memory and gave world media something to see. The reason everyone remembers Auschwitz and knows very little about the 2.3 million people murdered by the Nazis and buried in mass graves is that in the rural settings, there was nothing left behind other than fields and forests. The last known concentration camp was seen in Bosnia in 1992, but today killers have resorted to bombing, shooting, cutting their victims' throats, and burying them in mass graves. The victims disappear. It's what happened in Rwanda and Cambodia, and it's what ISIS did to the Yazidis in Iraq.

Father Patrick learned in Eastern Europe that it was not ideology and hate alone that attracted soldiers and killers to these movements. No matter the era or the country, genocide was built on three pillars:

1. Ideology
2. Sex
3. Money

It's challenging to retain a steady supply of workers, or killers, with ideology alone, which is why the sex and money are so important. The Nazis raped the Jewish women and stole their belongings. It's what fueled their efforts.

Father Patrick has said, "There are so many people fighting against us that we have no choice but to keep fighting. If not, we disappear." It's a human disease that he has dedicated his life to combating, yet he remains optimistic about the future. The fight continues for the next generation, but as the battleground shifts to online, he sees young people as the key to victory. He keeps returning to the story of Cain and Abel and feels compelled to search for the answers and the whereabouts of his brothers, be they his Jewish brothers in Eastern Europe or his Yazidi brothers in Iraq. He doesn't have a congregation; his work and his calling are his congregation.

Epilogue

It was nothing short of a miracle.

Tara and I married the week before Rosh Hashanah in September 2013. Like after any Jewish wedding, within minutes there was already talk of babies. Six years and eight rounds of IVF later, we learned that she was pregnant. It had been a long, emotional, and expensive roller coaster. Although I was still mourning the loss of my mother, life was good. We felt grateful and blessed, though cautious, so we decided not to tell anyone for at least three months. In our Sukkah, we first told my father and my aunt, an evening that was remarkably different from the Shabbos dinner spent alone with my father on Black Friday after the passing of my mother.

As we began to tell more friends, the darkness returned. The violence of Pittsburgh a year earlier had emerged in and around New York City. Pipe bombs, teenage fists, and machetes injured and killed our fellow Jews in the most diverse region of our country. My wife and I began to wonder what kind of world we were bringing a new Jewish life into. There was little reason for optimism, yet we remained hopeful.

As we entered the third trimester, the world entered a global pandemic. Even the leading infectious disease and public health experts could not predict what each week would bring. All we knew was that we were sailing into a very different reality. That reality didn't sink in until I was turned away at the front door of the hospital. Eight months into a relatively easy pregnancy, Tara began regular monitoring visits. I was eager to see clear images and video, but I was relegated to the car. The hospital and adjacent medical buildings were on lockdown. Only select patients were welcome, and I did not make the cut. One cold and rainy morning brought back memories of Black Friday and the Shabbos of the Pittsburgh massacre. Miserable, I was alone in the car and wondering, *What else will be different now?*

When Tara came back out, she presented me with a bottle of hand sanitizer and a sonogram photo, complete with hair, a little nose, and a thumb being sucked. We didn't want to know the sex of the baby, but as we sat with our emotions in the parking lot, the first thing that crossed our minds was that we were going to have this baby alone – no friends and no family – so if he were a boy, perhaps we could not even have a bris.

Passover arrived, and we sat alone in our dining room, staring at each other and looking at the art we had purchased the year prior when visiting Israel for Passover. That trip was a much-needed escape for both of us and an amazing chance to recharge after five months of mourning. Unforgettable memories in a country we love fell by the wayside as the tragedy in Poway unfolded. With these memories and emotions consuming us, it was easy to forget that Tara was ready to burst at any minute. Four glasses of wine helped me but could not help her.

There were never any false alarms. Tara didn't experience any morning sickness and was never exiled to being flat on her back. As the pandemic continued, despite Tara being eight months pregnant, we found ourselves going on long walks to explore the neighborhood where for years we'd watched other young parents teach their children how to ride bikes and throw footballs.

Then, on the rainy morning of Sunday, April 19, 2020, my wife, who is notoriously late for everything, was up early. We were going to have a baby – ten days earlier than planned.

We raced to the hospital only to be greeted by a new edition: a giant LED sign, normally reserved for a construction site on the highway, reading, "NO VISITORS." We had come this far and overcome so much that me missing out on the delivery of my first child was not an option. In an eerily empty lobby, I had to attest that I was indeed the father. We were suited up with PPE, now a household term, and told to stay in our room and religiously wash our hands. One by one, the doctors and nurses would visit as the day went on, but we could only make out their eye color, as they were suited up, ready for a pandemic rather than the most memorable experience of our lives.

After nearly twelve hours, Eliora Galit – named for my mother, Elisheva – joined our family. Our daughter's name loosely translates from Hebrew to a "wave of divine light." Despite the darkness and uncertainty around us and our Jewish community, her birth reminded us that life goes on and that we must always look for the light.

Over sleepless nights and a professional routine upended by a pandemic, this book ultimately materialized. The inability to physically join our Jewish community for daily prayer gave way to increased text study and virtual learning.

My life remains guided by traditional Judaism, the State of Israel, and the well-being of the American Jewish community. That was instilled in me by mother, and I hope to instill it in my daughter. I was reminded of that commitment every day when working on this book, be it in the early morning hours with the baby by my side or while conducting phone interviews during my commute to Washington before the pandemic.

The *Zohar* (Tazria 46a) relays the ancient story of Rabbi Chiya and Rabbi Yosi, two great sages deeply familiar with all aspects of Judaism. When they least expect it, they encounter a child on the side of the road who reminds the two wise elders of what they know. It is human nature to focus on the bad and to engage in negative talk. This is sinful. The child also reveals how we are punished when we have the ability and opportunity to relay good news and yet choose not to. Tradition teaches that upon hearing the wisdom of the child, the rabbis recite aloud Proverbs 4:18: "The path of the righteous is like the light of dawn; it shines ever brighter until the day is perfect."

Life has thrown me curveballs. There will always be antisemitism and personal speedbumps along the way. I do not know what "perfect" is for the Jewish people or where our path will take us in a post-pandemic world. However, when I least expected it, even while mourning and during a global pandemic, working on this book has allowed a little bit of light to continue to shine ever brighter.

May the father of all mercies scatter light, and not darkness, upon our paths, and make us all in our several vocations useful here, and in His own due time and way everlastingly happy.

President George Washington, "Letter to the Hebrew Congregation in Newport," August 1790

Acknowledgments

In traditional Judaism, the term for gratitude is *hakarat hatov.* However, the literal translation for this is "recognition of goodness." I had not given this distinction much thought until I began to think over all those who supported me and recognized the good that might come from such an undertaking.

The individuals profiled in the preceding pages were and are a source of inspiration. I will forever be grateful that they lent me their most valuable resource – their time. In some instances, our first conversation was one between strangers. As our discussions proceeded, they allowed me to ask diverse questions ranging from the personal to the philosophical. In February and March 2020, some interviews were in person. Before long, together we discovered the wonders of Zoom. Thanks. *Merci. Danke. Gracias. Hvala.*

There is a famous verse in the Mishnah, the first written compilation of Jewish literature from nearly two thousand years ago, that encourages all Jews, "Make for yourself a rabbi; acquire for yourself a friend."

Tradition teaches that the term *rabbi* is not just limited to someone who conducts prayer services and decides questions of law. A rabbi serves as a public role model for the community at large and is always accessible to those who hope to better the community. A friend, by contrast, is one who privately provides constructive criticism and candid advice.

There are two individuals who believed in this undertaking from day one. This has been possible only because of their insight and perspective. Throughout this, they have been my rabbis in the tradition of the Mishnah, and they have become friends in every sense of the term.

Stephen Schneider has roots in Oregon, now lives in Washington, and pre-pandemic was often traveling around the globe advocating on behalf of Israel and the Jewish community. I have fond memories from childhood of my first computer game, Oregon Trail. Writing this book felt like following a book trail, and Stephen was my guide on its many twists and turns. He made introductions, served as a sounding board, and provided motivation to continue forward when I needed it most.

Avi Jorisch calls Washington, DC, home, but is as comfortable in Jerusalem and other world capitals. Throughout this process, he opened my eyes in many ways – including to the Virginia backwoods and hikes along the Shenandoah Mountains. While working on this book, I read, reread, and then read again his 2018 book, *Thou Shalt Innovate*. Perhaps not three times, but I recommend you do too. His thoughts on researching, writing, and marketing have been invaluable. I will forever be grateful for this as well as his introduction to Gefen Publishing House.

Ilan Greenfield and his Jerusalem-based team at Gefen have made this dream a reality. Kezia Raffel Pride approached the editing process with surgical precision. Thank you to project managers Shiran Halimi and Daphne Abrahams for the incredible attention to detail. In the latter stages of this journey, their world was turned upside down by war for two long weeks in May 2021. Israelis are not only innovative, they are resilient. The entire Gefen team is no exception.

The historic summer of 2020 had me juggling the new adventures of fatherhood with ever-evolving professional obligations while working from home. Two women believed in the concept of this book and provided countless hours reviewing each profile and offering suggestions on how to capture the best story for the widest audience. Throughout this part of the process, they kept an eye on marketing. We often repeated, "Two Jews; five opinions." Most importantly, they had valuable tips on how to bond with my daughter during these formative first months. *Todah rabbah*, Rosalie Alter and Ellen Lightman. (And Richard and Noah too!)

In the final stages of this undertaking, Joshua Ehrich, Howard Friedman, Paula Joffe, Wayne Klitofsky, Marilyn Rosenthal, Betsy Sheerr, and Connie Smukler each were quite helpful.

Life changed in August 2020 when we met Channah Akkerman – more accurately, when our daughter met Channah. She has been an invaluable addition to our family.

Jewish tradition teaches that if it were not for women, the Jewish community would still be enslaved in Egypt. If it were not for my wife, this entire endeavor would not have been possible. She has approached the personal and professional hurdles we have faced together over the course of the last three years with patience and grace. Additionally, she embodies every attribute profiled in this book. She is a twenty-first-century "woman of valor."

Sources

Prologue

Scriptural translations: author's own.

Pittsburgh Post-Gazette. "A Portrait of the 'Darkest Day in Pittsburgh History.'" October 28, 2018. https://newsinteractive.post-gazette.com/photos/2018 /10/28/synagogue-shooting-squirrel-hill-pittsburgh-photos/.

Bush, George W. "George W. Bush Delivers Emotional Eulogy for His Father George H. W. Bush." *Wall Street Journal* YouTube page. December 5, 2018. https://www.youtube.com/watch?v=htPQrCBLBaQ.

Goldman, Chanie. "A Light unto the Nations." Chabad.org. https://www .chabad.org/library/article_cdo/aid/304867/jewish/A-Light-Unto-the -Nations.htm.

Haberman, Clyde. "Attack in Israel: The Scene; On the No. 5 Bus Line, A Thud, Then Silence." *New York Times*, October 20, 1994. https://www .nytimes.com/1994/10/20/world/attack-in-israel-the-scene-on-the-no -5-bus-line-a-thud-then-silence.html.

BBC Mundo. "Hallan muerto a Alberto Nisman, el fiscal que denunció a la presedentia de Argentina." January 19, 2015. https://www.bbc.com /mundo/ultimas_noticias/2015/01/150118_ultnot_argentina_muerte _fiscal_nisman_ng?ocid=socialflow_facebook.

Mittleman, Ari. "Your View: After Pittsburgh Synagogue Shooting, Perhaps Nation Can Embrace Bipartisan Unity." *Morning Call*, November 4, 2018. https://www.mcall.com/opinion/mc-opi-synagogue-shooting-pittsburgh -reflection-20181101-story.html.

Pascus, Brian, and Peter Martinez. "'We Need to Battle Darkness with Light': Rabbi Wounded in Attack Offers Inspiration." CBS News, April 29, 2019. https://www.cbsnews.com/news/deadly-chabad-poway-shooting -san-diego-lori-gilbert-kaye-rabbi-yisroel-goldstein-describes-attack/.

Robertson, Campbell, Christopher Mele, and Sabrina Tavernise. "11 Killed in Synagogue Massacre; Suspect Charged with 29 Counts." *New York Times*, October 27, 2018. https://www.nytimes.com/2018/10/27/us /active-shooter-pittsburgh-synagogue-shooting.html.

Aron, Melanie. "Kol Yisrael Arevim Zeh ba-Zeh, or Is It Zeh la-Zeh?" World Union for Progressive Judaism, April 23, 2017. https://wupj.org/library /the-weekly-portion/1095/kol-yisrael-arevim-zeh-ba-zeh-or-is-it-zeh-la -zeh-parashat-behar-bechukotai/.

Chabad.org. "Thirty-Six Aphorisms of the Baal Shem Tov." https://www .chabad.org/library/article_cdo/aid/3073/jewish/36-Aphorisms-of-the -Baal-Shem-Tov.htm.

Tal, Yaari. "Touro Synagogue." *Digital Encyclopedia of George Washington*. https://www.mountvernon.org/library/digitalhistory/digital-encyclopedia /article/touro-synagogue/.

Selk, Avi, Tim Craig, Shawn Boburg, and Andrew Ba Tran. "'They Showed His Photo, and My Stomach Just Dropped': Neighbors Recall Synagogue Massacre Suspect as Loner." *Washington Post*, October 29, 2018. https:// www.washingtonpost.com/nation/2018/10/28/victims-expected-be -named-after-killed-deadliest-attack-jews-us-history/.

Chapter 1

"2020 Population." NYC OpenData. Updated February 3, 2017. https:// data.cityofnewyork.us/City-Government/2020-population/t8c6-3i7b.

"About Aston." Aston Bright, accessed December 4, 2020. http://astonbright.com.

"About." National Fire and Rescue Authority, updated July 24, 2018. https:// www.gov.il/en/departments/about/aboutfireauthority.

Abuhewelia, Iyad, and Isabel Kershner. "He Played at Death in a Gaza Cemetery. Then He Was Buried There." *New York Times*, April 22, 2018. https://www.nytimes.com/2018/04/22/world/middleeast/gaza-protests .html.

Alarifi, Abdulaziz, Roth Phylaktou, and Gordon E. Andrews. "What Kills People in a Fire? Heat or Smoke?" 9th Saudi Students Conference, Birmingham, UK, February 2016. https://www.researchgate.net /publication/299080072_What_Kills_People_in_a_Fire_Heat_or _Smoke.

Gross, Judah Ari. "Israel Limits Entrance of Helium into Gaza after Balloons Scorch South." *Times of Israel*, June 12, 2018. https://www.timesofisrael .com/israel-limits-entrance-of-helium-into-gaza-after-balloons-scorch -south/.

Ben Zikri, Almog. "Fire Damage to Israel Agriculture Near Gaza Border Estimated at $1.4m and Rising." *Haaretz*, March 6, 2018. https://www .haaretz.com/israel-news/.premium.MAGAZINE-fire-damage-to-gaza -border-area-agriculture-estimated-at-1-4m-1.6140094.

Bernadino, Mike. "Mike Tyson Explains One of His Most Famous Quotes." *Sun Sentinel*, November 9, 2012. https://www.sun-sentinel.com/sports /fl-xpm-2012-11-09-sfl-mike-tyson-explains-one-of-his-most-famous -quotes-20121109-story.html.

Bronner, Ethan. "A Town under Fire Becomes a Symbol for Israel." *New York Times*, April 5, 2008. https://www.nytimes.com/2008/04/05/world /middleeast/05sderot.html.

Buckley, John. *Air Power in the Age of Total War*. Abingdon, UK: Routledge, 1998.

Einav, Hagai. "Aerial Firefighting Squadron Holds First Drill." Ynet, May 5, 2011. https://www.ynetnews.com/articles/0,7340,L-4065286,00.html.

Farrell, Stephen. "Why Is the U.S. Moving Its Embassy to Jerusalem?" Reuters, May 7, 2018. https://www.reuters.com/article/us-usa-israel

-diplomacy-jerusalem-explai/why-is-the-u-s-moving-its-embassy-to
-jerusalem-idUSKBN1I811N.

Fayyad, Huthifa. "Gaza's Great March of Return Protests Explained." Al
Jazeera, March 30, 2019. https://www.aljazeera.com/news/2019/3/30
/gazas-great-march-of-return-protests-explained.

"FAQ." Emergency Volunteer Project, accessed October 28, 2020. https://
www.evp.org.il/FAQ.html.

"Fire Growth & Flow-Rate." *3D Firefighting Safety Bulletin* 1 (July 4,
2007). http://911ready.org/documents/emergency_preparedness_docs
/Fire%20Growth%20and%20Flow%20Rate%20-%20Grimwood.pdf.

Fisher, Dan. "'Ancient Merits of Stone': Age-Old Architecture of Israel
Still Solid as a Rock." *Los Angeles Times*, June 13, 1985. https://www
.latimes.com/archives/la-xpm-1985-06-13-mn-10634-story.html#:~:
text=The%20Jerusalem%20holy%20places%20of,heaven%20to
%20confer%20with%20God.

Times of Israel. "Gazans Fly Kite with Petrol Bomb into Israel, Where It
Starts Fire in Field." April 15, 2018. https://www.timesofisrael.com
/gazans-fly-kite-with-petrol-bomb-into-israel-sets-field-afire/.

Times of Israel. "In Worst Blaze to Date, Gaza Fire Kites Destroy Vast Parts of
Nature Reserve." June 2, 2018. https://www.timesofisrael.com/palestinian
-fire-kites-destroy-much-of-nature-reserve-along-gaza-border/.

"Israel Population." Worldometer, accessed October 29, 2020. https://www
.worldometers.info/world-population/israel-population/.

Variety. "Israel Wins Eurovision Contest." May 12, 2018. https://variety.com/2018
/music/news/israel-eurovision-netta-toy-song-win-1202808622/.

Jaffe-Hoffman, Maayan. "Fire Kites Sting Negev Honey Farms Just before
Rosh Hashanah." Jewish News Syndicate, August 2, 2018. https://www
.jns.org/fire-kites-sting-negev-honey-farms-just-before-rosh-hashanah/.

Jeffrey, Adam. "Deadly Protests Erupt over the US Embassy Move to Jerusalem." CNBC, May 14, 2018. https://www.cnbc.com/2018/05/14 /deadly-protests-erupt-over-the-us-embassy-move-to-jerusalem.html.

"Jerusalem: Urban Characteristics and Major Trends in the City's Development." Israel Ministry of Foreign Affairs, August 25, 1999. https://www.mfa.gov.il/mfa/mfa-archive/1999/pages/municipal %20services%20in%20jerusalem%20-%20network%20of%20servi.aspx.

Keeler, Brett. "Containment Efforts Increase as West Mims Wildfire Grows." WUFT, April 19, 2017. https://www.wuft.org/news/2017/04/19/contain ment-efforts-increase-as-west-mims-wildfire-grows/.

Kellerman, Carol. "Racing to the Scene of the Wrong Emergency." *Gotham Gazette*, September 30, 2019. https://www.gothamgazette.com/opinion /8824-racing-to-the-scene-of-the-wrong-emergency.

Klein, Christopher. "Attack of Japan's Killer WWII Balloons, 70 Years Ago." History, May 5, 2015. https://www.history.com/news/attack-of -japans-killer-wwii-balloons-70-years-ago.

Times of Israel. "Large Fire Caused by Kite Sent from Gaza Rages outside Israeli Kibbutz." July 7, 2018. https://www.timesofisrael.com/large-fire -caused-by-kite-sent-from-gaza-rages-outside-israeli-kibbutz/.

"Melting Point Chart." Uniweld, accessed October 29, 2020. http://uniweld .com/resources/safety/melting-point-chart/.

Myre, Greg. "Israeli Withdrawal from Gaza Proceeds Faster Than Expected." *New York Times*, August 19, 2005. https://www.nytimes .com/2005/08/19/international/middleeast/israeli-withdrawal-from -gaza-proceeds-faster-than.html.

Times of Israel. "Over 1,000 Fires Ravage Israel over 3 Days, Forcing Evacuation of Thousands." May 26, 2019. https://www.timesofisrael .com/over-1000-fires-ravage-israel-over-3-days-forcing-evacuation-of -thousands/.

Rasgon, Adam. "Gaza Groups Say Border Protests to Stop until March, Resume Infrequently in 2020," *Times of Israel*, December 26, 2019. https://www.timesofisrael.com/gaza-groups-say-border-protests-to -stop-until-march-resume-infrequently-in-2020/.

Rinat, Zafrir. "Negev Tortoise Gets UN Attention amid Extinction Threat." *Haaretz*, August 8, 2020. https://www.haaretz.com/1.5027223.

Salah, Hana, and Noga Tarnopolsky. "They're Calling It the Kite War. How a Simple Plaything Became a Potent Weapon in the Gaza Strip." *Los Angeles Times*, June 18, 2018. https://www.latimes.com/world/la-fg-israel-gaza -kites-20180618-story.html.

Times of Israel. "Scorching July 2017 Was One of Israel's Hottest on Record." August 2, 2017. https://www.timesofisrael.com/scorching-july -2017-was-one-of-israels-hottest-on-record/.

"Sderot Factory Destroyed by Rocket Fire." Israel Ministry of Foreign Affairs, June 29, 2014. https://mfa.gov.il/MFA/ForeignPolicy/Terrorism/Pages /Sderot-factory-destroyed-by-rocket-fire-29-Jun-2014.aspx.

Sharett, Guy. "The Top 10 Hebrew Slang Words That You Should Learn." Culture Trip, February 9, 2017. https://theculturetrip.com/middle-east /israel/articles/the-top-10-hebrew-slang-words/.

Urquart, Conor, Ian Black, and Mark Tran. "Hamas Takes Control of Gaza." *Guardian*, June 15, 2007. https://www.theguardian.com/world/2007/jun /15/israel4.

"Vital Statistics: Latest Population Statistics for Israel." Jewish Virtual Library, accessed December 4, 2020. https://www.jewishvirtuallibrary .org/latest-population-statistics-for-israel.

"Wildfire 101: The Fire Triangle and the Fire Tetrahedron." Redzone, February 17, 2016. https://www.redzone.co/2016/02/17/wildfire-101 -the-fire-triangle-and-the-fire-tetrahedron/.

Zahavi, Adi. "First Responders with a Mission." Emergency Volunteers Project, accessed October 28, 2020. https://www.evp.org.il/First-Responders-With-A-Mission.html.

Zucchino, David. "Heroic Firefighter Is Alive – and Still on the Job." *Los Angeles Times*, September 22, 2001. https://www.latimes.com/archives/la-xpm-2001-sep-22-mn-48541-story.html.

Chapter 2

"1936–1945 Sachsenhausen Concentration Camp." Gedenkstätte und Museum Sachsenhausen, accessed November 5, 2020. https://www.sachsenhausen-sbg.de/en/history/1936-1945-sachsenhausen-concentration-camp/.

"About Us." Claims Conference, accessed November 5, 2020. http://www.claimscon.org/about/.

"Assessing Guilt." United States Holocaust Memorial Museum, accessed November 5, 2020. https://encyclopedia.ushmm.org/content/en/article/assessing-guilt.

Barr, Niall, MD. "Rommel in the Desert." BBC History, updated February 17, 2011. http://www.bbc.co.uk/history/worldwars/wwtwo/rommel_desert_01.shtml.

Beauchamp, Zack. "'Rent-a-Jew' Is an Actual Thing in Germany. And, Amazingly, It's a Good Idea." Vox, December 15, 2016. https://www.vox.com/world/2016/12/15/13958618/rent-a-jew-germany.

"Buchenwald." United States Holocaust Memorial Museum, accessed November 5, 2020. https://encyclopedia.ushmm.org/content/en/article/buchenwald.

Burleigh, Nina. "Haunting MoMa: The Forgotten Story of 'Degenerate' Dealer Alfred Flechtheim." *Observer*, February 14, 2012. https://observer.com/2012/02/haunting-moma-the-forgotten-story-of-degenerate-dealer-alfred-flechtheim/.

Butler, Desmond. "Germany Plans to Raise Status of Nation's Jews." *New York Times*, November 15, 2002. https://www.nytimes.com/2002/11/15/world/germany-plans-to-raise-status-of-nation-s-jews.html.

"Dachau Concentration Camp." History, updated January 27, 2020. https://www.history.com/topics/world-war-ii/dachau.

"East Germany: A Failed Experience in Dictatorship." DW. https://www.dw.com/en/east-germany-a-failed-experiment-in-dictatorship/a-50717157.

Eddy, Melissa. "How Dresden Looked after a World War II Firestorm 75 Years Ago." *New York Times*, updated February 14, 2020. https://www.nytimes.com/2020/02/13/world/europe/dresden-germany-anniversary.html.

"Education about National Socialism and the Holocaust." Learning from History, accessed November 5, 2020. http://learning-from-history.de/International/Posting/7474.

Reuters. "FACTBOX-Olympics-Past Boycotts and Cancellations." March 23, 2020. https://www.reuters.com/article/health-coronavirus-olympics/factbox-olympics-past-boycotts-and-cancellations-idUSL8N2BG3M2.

Flight, Tim. "This Is What Life Was Like in Communist East Germany." History Collection, December 18, 2019. https://historycollection.com/this-is-what-life-was-like-in-communist-east-germany/.

Grote, Michael H. "Foreign Banks' Attraction to the Financial Centre Frankfurt – An Inverted 'U'-Shaped Relationship." *Journal of Economic Geography* 8, no. 2 (March 2008): 239–58. https://www.jstor.org/stable/26161264.

"Holocaust Denial: Key Dates." United States Holocaust Memorial Museum, accessed November 5, 2020. https://encyclopedia.ushmm.org/content/en/article/holocaust-denial-key-dates.

"Holocaust Survivors Claim Compensation Bias." *Los Angeles Times*, May 8, 1995. https://www.latimes.com/archives/la-xpm-1995-05-08-mn-63818 -story.html.

Hulton, Michael. *Jewish, Gay & Avant-Garde in Nazi Germany: Uncle Alfred Flechtheim's Unexpected Legacies in Art, AIDS & Law.* Santa Barbara, CA: Keiran Publishing, 2018.

Knöfel, Ulrike. "US Congress Demands Actions on Nazi Looted Art." *Spiegel*, November 26, 2015. https://www.spiegel.de/international/germany/bava rian-museums-reluctant-to-return-nazi-looted-art-a-1064113.html.

"Kristallnacht." History, updated December 6, 2018. https://www.history .com/topics/holocaust/kristallnacht.

Ladd, Brian. *The Ghosts of Berlin: Confronting Germany History in the Urban Landscape.* Chicago: University of Chicago Press, 1997.

"Looted Art." United States Holocaust Memorial Museum, accessed November 5, 2020. https://www.ushmm.org/collections/bibliography/looted-art.

Morrison, Jim. "The True Story of the Monuments Men." *Smithsonian*, February 7, 2014. https://www.smithsonianmag.com/history/true-story -monuments-men-180949569/.

Rothfeld, Anne. "Nazi Looted Art: The Holocaust Records Project." *Prologue Magazine* 34, no. 2 (Summer 2002), https://www.archives.gov /publications/prologue/2002/summer/nazi-looted-art-1.html.

Niemtzow, Josh. "The Realization of Comprehensive Holocaust Education in West Germany." Emory College of Arts and Sciences, July 2015. https:// www.researchgate.net/publication/307560009_The_Realization_of _Comprehensive_Holocaust_Education_in_West_Germany.

"November 9/10, 1938, A Synagogue in Flames in Siegen, Germany, during Kristallnacht." Yad Vashem: The World Holocaust Remembrance Center, accessed November 5, 2020. https://www.yadvashem.org /holocaust/this-month/november/1938-2.html.

"Nuremberg Race Laws." United States Holocaust Memorial Museum, accessed November 5, 2020. https://encyclopedia.ushmm.org/content/en/article/nuremberg-laws.

"Population in the Former Territories of the Federal Republic of Germany and the German Democratic Republic from 1995 to 2016." Statista, accessed November 5, 2020. https://www.statista.com/statistics/1054199/population-of-east-and-west-germany/.

Pruitt, Sarah. "When Hitler Tried (and Failed) to Be an Artist." History, September 13, 2019. https://www.history.com/news/adolf-hitler-artist-paintings-vienna.

Rosenberg, Matt. "Germany's Capital Moved from Bonn to Berlin." Thought Co, July 28, 2019. https://www.thoughtco.com/germany-capital-from-bonn-to-berlin-1434930.

Schwarz, Géraldine. "My Family Has a Nazi Past. I See That Ideology Returning across Europe." *Guardian*, April 18, 2018. https://www.theguardian.com/commentisfree/2018/apr/18/family-nazi-past-ideology-europe-germany-fascism-far-right

Schymura, Yvonne. "The Soldiers Who Saved Europe's Art from Hitler." ABC News, December 8, 2013. https://abcnews.go.com/International/soldiers-saved-europes-art-hitler/story?id=21122199.

"Staatsexamen." Uni Assist, accessed November 4, 2020. https://www.uni-assist.de/en/tools/glossary-of-terms/description/details/staatsexamen/.

Stanska, Zuzanna. "The Story of Unrealized Hitler's Art Museum in Linz." *DailyArt*, May 27, 2017. https://www.dailyartmagazine.com/story-hitlers-art-museum/.

George Clooney, dir. *The Monuments Men*. Los Angeles, CA: Columbia Pictures/Fox 2000 Pictures, 2014.

"Looted Art." United States Holocaust Memorial Museum, accessed November 5, 2020. https://www.ushmm.org/collections/bibliography/looted-art.

"The Monuments Men in April 1945: Siegen, Finally." National Archives, August 25, 2015. https://text-message.blogs.archives.gov/2015/08/25/monuments-men-april-1945-siegen/.

"The Real Monuments Men." National Archives, February 6, 2014. https://unwritten-record.blogs.archives.gov/2014/02/06/the-real-monuments-men/.

"The Reunification of Germany: Helmut Kohl and the Struggles of Reunification." Britannica, accessed November 5, 2020. https://www.britannica.com/place/Germany/Helmut-Kohl-and-the-struggles-of-reunification.

"The Unification Treaty between the FRG and the GDR (Berlin, 31 August, 1990)." CVCE, September 24, 2012. https://reparations.qub.ac.uk/assets/uploads/1990-Unification-Treaty-Germany.pdf.

"V-E Day is celebrated in America and Britain." History, accessed November 6, 2020. https://www.history.com/this-day-in-history/victory-in-europe.

"Washington Conference Principles on Nazi-Confiscated Art." US Department of State, accessed November 6, 2020. https://www.state.gov/washington-conference-principles-on-nazi-confiscated-art/.

Westergaard Madsen, Jacob. "The Vividness of the Past: A Retrospect on the West German *Historikerstreit* in the Mid-1980s." *University of Sussex Journal of Contemporary History* 1 (2000): 1–9. https://core.ac.uk/download/pdf/2709461.pdf.

"World War Two and Germany, 1939–1945." BBC Bitesize, accessed November 5, 2020. https://www.bbc.co.uk/bitesize/guides/zwrfj6f/revision/5.

Chapter 3

"Apartheid." History, updated March 3, 2020. https://www.history.com/topics/africa/apartheid#:~:text=Apartheid%20(%E2%80%9Capart ness%E2%80%9D)%20in%20the,existing%20policies%20of%20 racial%20segregation.

Haaretz. "Desmond Tutu: U.S. Christians Must Recognize Israel as Apartheid State." June 17, 2014. https://www.haaretz.com/tutu-israel-is-apartheid-state-1.5252256.

Erlanger, Steven, and Isabel Kershner. "Israel and Hamas Trade Attacks as Tension Rises." *New York Times*, July 8, 2014. https://www.nytimes.com/2014/07/09/world/middleeast/israel-steps-up-offensive-against-hamas-in-gaza.html.

Fisher, Max. "'The Last Great Liberator': Why Mandela Made and Stayed Friends with Dictators." *Washington Post*, December 10, 2013. https://www.washingtonpost.com/news/worldviews/wp/2013/12/10/the-last-great-liberator-why-mandela-made-and-stayed-friends-with-dictators/.

"Israel Launches Operation Protective Edge in Gaza Strip." NBC News, July 8, 2014. https://www.nbcnews.com/storyline/middle-east-unrest/israel-launches-operation-protective-edge-gaza-strip-n150281.

"Israel Reacts Angrily to Hamas Leader's Visit to South Africa." Middle East Eye, October 20, 2015. https://www.middleeasteye.net/news/israel-reacts-angrily-hamas-leaders-visit-south-africa.

Jacobs, Sean. "To So Many Africans, Fidel Castro Is a Hero. Here's Why." *Guardian*, November 30, 2016. https://www.theguardian.com/commentisfree/2016/nov/30/africa-fidel-castro-nelson-mandela-cuba.

Associated Press. "Mandela Arrives in Tehran, Lays Wreath at Khomeini Shrine." July 21, 1992. https://apnews.com/article/ad81cee784fd0130a2aaafa8aace9997.

Mandela, Nelson. *Long Walk to Freedom: The Autobiography of Nelson Mandela.* New York: Back Bay Books, 1995.

Musodoza, Masimba. "Remembering Golda Meir's African Legacy." *Times of Israel*, May 7, 2016. https://blogs.timesofisrael.com/remembering-golda-meirs-african-legacy/.

"Nelson Mandela." Britannica, accessed November 12, 2020. https://www.britannica.com/biography/Nelson-Mandela.

"Operation Protective Edge: July–August 2014." ADL, November 12, 2020. https://www.adl.org/resources/glossary-terms/operation-protective-edge-july-august-2014.

"Operation Protective Edge: The Facts." Israel Ministry of Foreign Affairs, accessed November 12, 2020. https://mfa.gov.il/MFA/ForeignPolicy/FAQ/Pages/Operation-Protective-Edge-The-facts.aspx.

"Our Mission." Club Z, accessed November 12, 2020. https://clubz.org/our-mission/.

Prusher, Ilene. "Mandela Was Critical of Occupation, but Fully Endorsed Israel's Right to Exist." *Haaretz*, December 9, 2013. https://www.haaretz.com/.premium-mandela-tough-but-fair-on-israel-1.5298232.

Quist-Arcton, Offeibea. "South Africans Reflect on Mandela's 'Rainbow Nation.'" NPR, December 13, 2013. https://www.npr.org/2013/12/13/250734816/south-africans-reflect-on-mandela-s-rainbow-nation.

Shilon, Avi. "Why Israel Supported South Africa's Apartheid Regime." *Haaretz*, updated April 10, 2018. https://www.haaretz.com/opinion/.premium-why-israel-supported-apartheid-regime-1.5298552.

"South African Jewish Community Welcomes 15-Year Low in Antisemitic Incidents." World Jewish Congress, February 11, 2020. https://www.worldjewishcongress.org/en/news/south-african-jewish-community-proud-to-note-15-year-low-in-antisemitic-incidents-2-4-2020.

Jerusalem Post. "Thousands Gather in South Africa to Show Support for Israel." August 4, 2014. https://www.jpost.com/operation-protective-edge/thousands-gather-in-south-africa-to-show-support-for-israel-369952.

"Water Access in South Africa." Massachusetts Institute of Technology, accessed November 12, 2020. http://12.000.scripts.mit.edu/mission2017/case-studies/water-access-in-south-africa/#:~:text=Currently%2C%20South%20Africa%20has%20a,household%20per%20month%20%5B5%5D.

Chapter 4

"Axis Invasion of Yugoslavia." United States Holocaust Memorial Museum, accessed November 6, 2020. https://encyclopedia.ushmm.org/content /en/article/axis-invasion-of-yugoslavia.

"Balkans War: A Brief Guide." BBC News, March 18, 2016. https:// www.bbc.com/news/world-europe-17632399#:~:text=The%20war %20ended%20in%201995,bound%20by%20a%20central%20 government.

"Bilateralni odnosi." Republika Hrvatska: Ministarstvo vanjskih i europskih poslova, accessed November 4, 2020. http://www.mvep.hr/hr/vanjska -politika/bilateralni-odnosi/datumi-priznanja/.

"Bio." Dr. Michael Baden, accessed November 6, 2020. https://www .drmichaelbaden.com/bio/.

"Biography." The Office of Dragan Primorac, accessed November 6, 2020. https://draganprimorac.org/biography/.

Butcher, Mike. "Israeli BC Pitango Launches Its 7th Early-Stage Fund of $175m." Tech Crunch, December 13, 2016. https://techcrunch .com/2016/12/13/israeli-vc-pitango-launches-its-7th-early-stage-fund -of-175m/.

"Caesarea." Britannica, accessed November 7, 2020. https://www.britannica .com/place/Caesarea.

"Concentration Camps: Jasenovac." Jewish Virtual Library, accessed November 6, 2020. https://www.jewishvirtuallibrary.org/jasenovac-camp.

Chemi Peres, LinkedIn profile, accessed November 6, 2020. https://www .linkedin.com/in/chemiperes/.

Jewish Telegraphic Agency. "Croatian President Goes to Israel." October 29, 2001. https://www.jta.org/2001/10/29/default/croatian-president-goes -to-israel.

"Croatia: Organisation of the Education System and of Its Structure." European Commission, December 17, 2019. https://eacea.ec.europa .eu/national-policies/eurydice/content/organisation-education -system-and-its-structure-14_en.

"Croatia Population." Worldometer, accessed November 10, 2020. https:// www.worldometers.info/world-population/croatia-population/.

"David Elazar (1925–1976)." Jewish Virtual Library, accessed November 7, 2020. https://www.jewishvirtuallibrary.org/elazar-david.

"Diplomatic Missions and Consular Offices of Croatia: State of Israel (The)." Republic of Croatia Ministry of Foreign Affairs, accessed November 4, 2020. http://www.mvep.hr/en/diplomatic-directory/israel-tel-aviv,153 .html.

"Dr. Henry Lee." The Henry C. Lee Institute of Forensic Science, accessed November 6, 2020. http://www.henryleeinstitute.com/about/dr-henry -lee/.

Fathi, Nazila. "Wipe Israel 'Off the Map.'" *New York Times*, October 27, 2005. https://www.nytimes.com/2005/10/27/world/africa/wipe-israel-off-the -map-iranian-says.html.

Fuoco, Michael A. "Famed Criminalist Henry Lee Recounts O. J. Simpson Trial." *Pittsburgh Post-Gazette*, June 1, 2017. https:// www.post-gazette.com/local/city/2017/06/02/criminalist-Henry -Lee-O-J-Simpson-trial-Duquesne-University/stories/201706020110.

Green, David B. "From Friends to Foes: How Israel and Iran Turned into Arch-Enemies." *Haaretz*, May 8, 2018. https://www.haaretz.com /middle-east-news/iran/MAGAZINE-how-israel-and-iran-went-from -allies-to-enemies-1.6049884.

Greif, Gideon. *Jasenovac: Auschwitz of the Balkans*. Belgrade: Knjiga komerc, 2018.

Reuters. "Haim Bar-Lev Dies; Israeli General, 69." *New York Times*, May 8, 1994. https://www.nytimes.com/1994/05/08/obituaries/haim-bar-lev -dies-israeli-general-69.html.

Hershberg, James G. "The Soviet Bloc and the Aftermath of the June 1967 War." Wilson Center, accessed November 6, 2020. https://www.wilsoncenter .org/publication/the-soviet-bloc-and-the-aftermath-the-june-1967-war.

"History of Croatia." Visit Croatia, accessed November 6, 2020. https://www .visit-croatia.co.uk/about-croatia/history-of-croatia/.

Hitchcock, Mark. *Iran and Israel: Wars and Rumors of Wars*. Eugene, OR: Harvest House Publishers, 2013.

Kuwait News Agency (KUNA). "Iranian President Visits Croatia." March 7, 2005. https://www.kuna.net.kw/ArticleDetails.aspx?language=en&id=1556943.

Isby, David C., ed. *Balkan Battlegrounds: A Military History of the Yugoslav Conflict, 1990–1995*. Langley, VA: Central Intelligence Agency, 2002.

"Israel." History, updated May 14, 2019. https://www.history.com/topics /middle-east/history-of-israel.

Times of Israel. "Israeli Embassies around the World Shut as Diplomats, Military Attachés Strike." October 30, 2019. https://www.timesofisrael .com/israeli-embassies-around-the-world-shut-as-diplomats-military -attaches-strike/.

"Israel International Relations: International Recognition of Israel." Jewish Virtual Library, accessed November 7, 2020. https://www .jewishvirtuallibrary.org/international-recognition-of-israel.

"Jewish Synagogue." Go Dubrovnik Guide, accessed November 6, 2020. https://www.godubrovnik.guide/dubrovnikthingstodo/jewish-synagogue/.

Kantrowitz, Anita. "Jewish Journal. Finding Jewels of Judaism on Italy's Adriatic Coast." Centro Primo Levi, accessed November 6, 2020. https://primolevicenter.org/jewish-journal-finding-jewels-of-judaism -on-italys-adriatic-coast/.

Kuwait News Agency (KUNA). "Khatami: Iran-Croatia Cooperation Can Boost Peace in the Mideast, Europe." May 20, 2003. https://www.kuna.net.kw/articledetails.aspx?id=1347300&language=en.

Lewis, Paul. "U.N. Repeals Its '75 Resolution Equating Zionism with Racism." *New York Times*, December 17, 1991. https://www.nytimes.com/1991/12/17/world/un-repeals-its-75-resolution-equating-zionism-with-racism.html

"Message from the Honorary President." Croatian-Israeli Business Club, accessed November 10, 2020. https://cibc.hr.

"Moses S. Schanfield: Curriculum Vitae." Accessed December 4, 2020. https://anthropology.columbian.gwu.edu/sites/g/files/zaxdzs1781/f/downloads/Schanfield2014.pdf.

Jewish Telegraph. "Nasser Arrives in Yugoslavia; Will Discuss Middle East with Tito, Nehru." July 13, 1956. https://www.jta.org/1956/07/13/archive/nasser-arrives-in-yugoslavia-will-discuss-middle-east-with-tito-nehru.

Phillips, Mitch. "France '98 – When Croatia Crashed the World Cup Party." Reuters, July 14, 2018. https://www.reuters.com/article/us-soccer-world-cup-final-1998/france-98-when-croatia-crashed-the-world-cup-party-idUSKBN1K40FT.

Primorac, Dragan. "Back in the fold. Modernizing Croatian science and education." *EMBO Reports* 9, no. 7 (July 2008): 596–99. https://www.ncbi.nlm.nih.gov/pmc/articles/PMC2475323/.

"Romanov Remains Identified using DNA." History, July 9, 1993. https://www.history.com/this-day-in-history/romanov-remains-identified.

Roth, Mandy. "How Israel Does Healthcare Innovation; An Insider's Look for Americans." Health Leaders, August 16, 2019. https://www.healthleadersmedia.com/innovation/how-israel-does-healthcare-innovation-insiders-look-americans.

Al Jazeera. "Sharon: No Jews in Gaza." February 2, 2004. https://www.aljazeera.com/news/2004/2/2/sharon-no-jews-in-gaza.

Slaus, Mario. "Dental Identification of War Victims from Petrinja in Croatia." *International Journal of Legal Medicine* 110, no. 2 (February 1997): 47–51. https://doi.org/10.1007/s004140050029.

"Split Jewish Heritage." Croatia Traveller, accessed November 6, 2020. https://www.croatiatraveller.com/central%20dalmatia/Split/Jewish-Heritage.html.

Sudetic, Chuck. "Deadly Clash in a Yugoslav Republic." *New York Times*, April 1, 1991. https://www.nytimes.com/1991/04/01/world/deadly-clash-in-a-yugoslav-republic.html.

"Suicide Bombing of Egged Bus No. 14A in Jerusalem." Israel Ministry of Foreign Affairs, February 22, 2004. http://www.israel.org/MFA/MFA-Archive/2004/Pages/Suicide%20bombing%20of%20Egged%20bus%20no.%2014A%20in%20Jerusalem%20-%2022-Feb-2004.aspx.

"SWC Israel Director Meets Croatian President Stjepan Mesíc in Jerusalem." Simon Wiesenthal Center, March 17, 2005. http://www.wiesenthal.com/about/news/swc-israel-director-meets.html.

Associated Press. "President Katsav Tours Dubrovnik as Part of Visit to Croatia." *Haaretz*, July 11, 2003. https://www.haaretz.com/1.5495829.

"The Breakup of Yugoslavia, 1990–1992." US Department of State: Office of the Historian, accessed November 6, 2020. https://history.state.gov/milestones/1989-1992/breakup-yugoslavia#:~:text=Secretary%20of%20State%20James%20Baker,independence%20on%20June%2025%2C%201991.

"The Jewish Community of Dubrovnik." Museum of the Jewish People at Beit Hatfutsot, accessed November 6, 2020. https://www.bh.org.il/jewish-community-dubrovnik/.

"Tito." Yad Vashem, accessed November 6, 2020. https://www.yadvashem.org/odot_pdf/Microsoft%20Word%20-%206270.pdf.

"Translational Medicine – Israel." Wohl Legacy, accessed November 6, 2020. https://www.wohl.org.uk/project/hadassah-medical-organisation-and -sheba-medical-centre-israel-wohl-institutes-for-translational-medicine/.

"Venture Capitalist Chemi Peres: Building a Vehicle to Finance Entrepreneurial Dreams." Wharton University of Pennsylvania, May 10, 2013. https://knowledge.wharton.upenn.edu/article/venture-capitalist -chemi-peres-building-a-vehicle-to-finance-entrepreneurial-dreams/.

"Yael Rubenstein: Curriculum Vitae." Accessed November 6, 2020. https://embassies.gov.il/singapore/NewsAndEvents/EventsgVisual /Curriculum%20Vitae.pdf.

Chapter 5

"Butterfly Group Restructures with New Partnerships." Christian Retailing, March 21, 2004. https://www.christianretailing.com/index.php/newsletter /previous-issues/51-industry-news/8742-butterfly-group-restructures-with -new-partnerships.

Diener, Bob. "Guatemala Loves Israel – The Inside Story." *Jerusalem Post*, January 4, 2020. https://www.jpost.com/opinion/guatemala-loves-israel -the-inside-story-613109.

Fisher, Ian. "Netanyahu Says U.S. Embassy 'Needs to Be' in Jerusalem." *New York Times*, January 29, 2017. https://www.nytimes.com/2017/01/29 /world/middleeast/benjamin-netanyahu-israel-jerusalem-embassy.html.

"Guatemala." The World Bank, accessed December 4, 2020. https://data .worldbank.org/country/GT.

"Guatemala Population." Worldometer, accessed November 10, 2020. https:// www.worldometers.info/world-population/guatemala-population/.

Heller, Jeffrey, and Dan Williams. "Guatemala Opens Embassy in Jerusalem, Two Days after U.S. Move." Reuters, May 16, 2018. https://www .reuters.com/article/us-israel-palestinians-guatemala/guatemala-opens -embassy-in-jerusalem-two-days-after-u-s-move-idUSKCN1IH0Q7.

"Israel International Relations: International Recognition of Israel." Jewish Virtual Library, accessed December 4, 2020. https://www.jewishvirtuallibrary.org/international-recognition-of-israel.

"Israel's Diplomatic Missions Abroad: Status of Relations." Israel Ministry of Foreign Affairs, accessed December 4, 2020. https://mfa.gov.il/mfa/abouttheministry/pages/israel-s%20diplomatic%20missions%20abroad.aspx.

"Jewish Population in the United States by State (1899–Present)." Jewish Virtual Library, accessed November 10, 2020. https://www.jewishvirtuallibrary.org/jewish-population-in-the-united-states-by-state.

Jimmy Morales, Facebook post. December 24, 2017. https://www.facebook.com/JimmyOficial/photos/a.521885541216591.1073741847.158778054194010/1768695479868918/?type=3&theater.

JTA, "Latin American Jews Honor Guatemalan Government for Teaching Holocaust Studies." *Times of Israel*, December 20, 2017. https://www.timesofisrael.com/latin-american-jews-honor-guatemalan-government-for-teaching-holocaust-studies/.

"Lior Haiat." IAC National Summit, accessed November 10, 2020. https://www.israeliamerican.org/iac-national-conference/team-member/lior-haiat.

"Pacaya." Smithsonian Institution: National Museum of Natural History, Global Volcanism Program, accessed November 10, 2020. https://volcano.si.edu/volcano.cfm?vn=342110.

"President Donald J. Trump Keeps His Promise to Open U.S. Embassy in Jerusalem, Israel." White House, May 14, 2018. Archived at https://www.jewishvirtuallibrary.org/donald-trump-administration-u-s-embassy-opening-in-jerusalem.

"President Rivlin Hosts State Dinner in Honor of Guatemalan President Morales." Israel Ministry of Foreign Affairs, November 28, 2016. https://mfa.gov.il/MFA/PressRoom/2016/Pages/President-Rivlin-hosts-state-dinner-in-honor-of-Guatemalan-President-Morales-28-November-2016.aspx.

"PM Netanyahu Meets with Guatemalan President Morales." Israel Ministry of Foreign Affairs, November 29, 2016. https://mfa.gov.il/MFA/PressRoom /2016/Pages/PM-Netanyahu-meets-with-Guatemalan-President -Morales-29-November-2016.aspx.

Rosenberg, David. "Guatemala: Israel Is a 'Light unto Nations.'" Arutz Sheva, May 16, 2018. https://www.israelnationalnews.com/News/News.aspx /246055.

Svirsky, Ronit. "A Suite for King David." Ynet, June 12, 2006. https://www .ynetnews.com/articles/0,7340,L-3335930,00.html.

"United States." The World Bank, accessed December 4, 2020. https://data .worldbank.org/country/united-states.

Chapter 6

"2019 AIPAC Policy Conference Draws over 18,000 Attendees." VIVA, accessed November 12, 2020. https://www.vivacreative.com/design-labs /aipac/.

"About Labour Friends of Israel." Labour Friends of Israel, accessed November 11, 2020. https://www.lfi.org.uk/about/.

"About Us." International March of the Living, accessed November 12, 2020. https://www.motl.org/about/.

"A Guide to Labour Party Anti-Semitism Claims." BBC News, October 29, 2020. https://www.bbc.com/news/uk-politics-45030552.

Ahren, Raphael. "Ex-Labour MP Who Got Rats on Doorstep Says Now's Time to Tackle Anti-Semitism." *Times of Israel*, December 16, 2019. https:// www.timesofisrael.com/ex-labour-mp-who-got-rats-on-doorstep-says -nows-time-to-tackle-anti-semitism/.

Allin, Simon. "Enfield Has Highest Serious Youth Violence Rate in London." *Enfield Independent*, January 4, 2019. https://www.enfield independent.co.uk/news/17335560.enfield-highest-serious-youth

-violence-rate-london/#:~:text=Enfield%20has%20the%20highest%20 rate,increase%20on%20the%20previous%20year.

Allin, Simon. "More Cuts Approved at Enfield Council," *Enfield Independent*. October 19, 2018. https://www.enfieldindependent.co.uk /news/16994476.cuts-approved-enfield-council/.

Times of Israel. "Citing Anti-Semitism, UK Labour Friend of Israel Head Is 8th MP to Quit Party." February 20, 2019. https://www.timesofisrael.com /eighth-lawmaker-quits-uks-labour-over-anti-semitism-and-brexit/.

Craig, Jon. "Three Amigos Launch Had Spark but Independent Group Needs a Big Hitter." Sky News, February 20, 2019. https://news.sky .com/story/three-amigos-launch-had-spark-but-independent-group -needs-a-big-hitter-11642915.

"Death Marches." Jewish Virtual Library, accessed November 12, 2020. https://www.jewishvirtuallibrary.org/death-marches.

"Death Marches." United States Holocaust Memorial Museum, accessed November 12, 2020. https://encyclopedia.ushmm.org/content/en/article /death-marches.

Doherty, Rosa. "Al Jazeera's Documentary Is Intended to 'Deny and Belittle the Serious Problem of Antisemitism Experienced by the Labour Party.'" *JC*, January 13, 2017. https://www.thejc.com/news/uk /al-jazeera-s-documentary-1.430595.

"Enfield's Violent Crime Rate Doubles in Seven Years." *Enfield Dispatch*, January 2, 2019. https://enfielddispatch.co.uk/enfields-violent-crime -rate-doubles-in-seven-years/.

"Foreign Terrorist Organizations." US Department of State, accessed November 11, 2020. https://www.state.gov/foreign-terrorist-organizations/.

"Former Labour MP Joan Ryan Urges People Not to Vote for Jeremy Corbyn." ITV, December 5, 2019. https://www.itv.com/news/2019-12-05/former -labour-mp-joan-ryan-becomes-latest-party-member-to-urge -people-not-to-vote-for-jeremy-corbyn.

"'From Holocaust to Redemption,' Rivlin to Lead 30th March of the Living." International March of the Living, April 8, 2018. https://www.motl.org/from-holocaust-to-redemption-rivlin-to-lead-30th-march-of-the-living/.

"Hendon: Judaism." British History Online, accessed November 11, 2020. https://www.british-history.ac.uk/vch/middx/vol5/p43.

Times of Israel. "Iranian Official Welcomes Jeremy Corbyn Win." September 19, 2015. https://www.timesofisrael.com/iranian-official-welcomes-jeremy-corbyn-win/.

"Joan Ryan." BBC News, October 17, 2002. http://news.bbc.co.uk/2/hi/uk_news/politics/2079485.stm.

Joan Ryan (@joanryanEnfield). Twitter. September 7, 2018, 1:17 a.m. https://twitter.com/joanryanEnfield/status/1037827090723340289.

Joan Ryan (@joanryanEnfield). Twitter. February 20, 2019, 12:07 a.m. https://twitter.com/joanryanEnfield/status/1097980964163276803.

"Labour Friends of Israel Chair Joan Ryan Loses No-Confidence Vote." Middle East Eye, September 7, 2018. https://www.middleeasteye.net/news/labour-friends-israel-chair-joan-ryan-loses-no-confidence-vote.

"Last Jews in the Last Months of the German Reich." Yad Vashem, accessed November 12, 2020. https://www.yadvashem.org/holocaust/about/end-of-war-aftermath/last-months.html.

Lewis, Helen. "Why British Jews Are Worried by Jeremy Corbyn." *The Atlantic,* December 10, 2019. https://www.theatlantic.com/international/archive/2019/12/british-jews-are-worried-jeremy-corbyn-and-labour-party/603259/.

Lewis, Tim. "From Nazi Camps to the Lake District: The Story of the Windermere Children." *Guardian,* January 5, 2020. https://www.theguardian.com/tv-and-radio/2020/jan/05/windermere-children-arek-hersh-survivor-bbc-drama.

"London Borough of Enfield: Child Poverty Needs Assessment; Executive Summary." Enfield Council, March 2011. https://governance.enfield.gov.uk/documents/s17174/.

Mccann, Kate. "Jeremy Corbyn Refuses to Denounce Terrorist 'Friends' Hamas and Hizbollah." *Telegraph*, May 2, 2016. https://www.telegraph.co.uk/news/2016/05/01/jeremy-corbyn-under-pressure-to-denounce-friends-hamas-and-hezbo/.

McGuinness, Alan. "Antisemitism 'Intimately Related' to Labour's Politics, Says MP Who Quit Party." Sky News, March 3, 2019. https://news.sky.com/story/antisemitism-intimately-related-to-labours-politics-says-mp-who-quit-party-11653947.

"Memorial Dedication for Bevin Boys WWII's 'Forgotten People.'" BBC News, April 11, 2013. https://www.bbc.com/news/av/uk-england-22105882.

Mendick, Robert. "Jeremy Corbyn's 10-Year Association with Group Which Denies the Holocaust." *Telegraph*, May 20, 2017. https://www.telegraph.co.uk/news/2017/05/20/jeremy-corbyns-10-year-association-group-denies-holocaust/.

"MP Joan Ryan Quits Labour for Independent Group." BBC News, February 20, 2019. https://www.bbc.com/news/uk-politics-47300832.

"Questions about Joining." Labour, accessed November 12, 2020. https://labour.org.uk/members/questions-about-joining/.

Rallings, Colin, and Michael Thrasher. "London Borough of Barnet Election Results, 1964–2010." The Elections Centre, accessed November 11, 2020. http://www.electionscentre.co.uk/wp-content/uploads/2015/06/Barnet-1964-2010.pdf.

Sheffield, Emma. "Seventy Years On." The National Holocaust Centre and Museum, accessed November 12, 2020. https://www.holocaust.org.uk/blog/70-years-on.

"Tarnow: History of the Community." [In Polish.] Wirtualny Szetl, accessed November 12, 2020. https://sztetl.org.pl/pl/miejscowosci/t/625-tarnow /99-historia-spolecznosci/138152-historia-spolecznosci.

"Westminster Attack: What Happened." BBC News, April 7, 2017. https:// www.bbc.com/news/uk-39355108.

"Westminster Terror attack: Who Were the Victims?" BBC News, October 3, 2018. https://www.bbc.com/news/uk-39363933.

Wiesel, Elie. Cited in Alvin P. Sanoff, "One Must Not Forget." *U.S. News and World Report*, October 27, 1986.

"What is BDS?" BDS, accessed November 12, 2020. https://bdsmovement.net /what-is-bds.

Chapter 7

"2017 Top 60 Schools by Jewish Population," Hillel International, March 15, 2018, https://www.hillel.org/about/news-views/news-views---blog /news-and-views/2018/03/15/2017-top-60-schools-by-jewish -population.

Schwartzman, Alec. "Matisyahu to Headline 'Declare Your Freedom' Festival." *Tulane Hullabaloo*, April 8, 2015. https://tulanehullabaloo.com/2191 /arcade/matisyahu-to-headline-declare-your-freedom-festival/.

Goldman, Ari L. "Dalai Lama Meets Jews from 4 Major Branches." *New York Times*, September 26, 1989. https://www.nytimes.com/1989/09/26 /nyregion/dalai-lama-meets-jews-from-4-major-branches.html.

"BDS Movement Growing in US Universities: Israel Campus Coalition." The New Arab, November 6, 2019. https://english.alaraby.co.uk/english /news/2019/11/6/report-shows-surge-in-bds-campaigns-on-us -campuses.

Beit Hatfutsot. "Dalí and Judaism – A Mysterious Relationship." Museum of the Jewish People, October 24, 2017. https://www.bh.org.il/blog-items /dali-judaism-mysterious-relationship/.

Jewish Telegraphic Agency. "Congress Leaders Do Not Approve Committee of Inquiry on Ford's Charges." December 27, 1926. https://www.jta .org/1926/12/27/archive/congress-leaders-do-not-approve-committee -of-in-quiry-on-fords-charges.

Robenstine, Clark. "French Colonial Policy and the Education of Women and Minorities: Louisiana in the Early Eighteenth Century." History of Education Quarterly 32, no. 2 (1992): 193–211. https://doi.org/10 .2307/368985.

Dor-Shav, Ethan. "Ecclesiastes: Fleeting and Timeless." *Azure* 18 (2004). https://mosaicmagazine.com/observation/history-ideas/2004/10 /ecclesiastes-fleeting-and-timeless/.

Sherwood, Harriet. "Five Members of Jewish Family Killed in Suspected Palestinian Militant Attack." *Guardian*, March 12, 2011. https://www .theguardian.com/world/2011/mar/12/west-bank-jewish-family-killed.

"History of New Orleans." New Orleans, accessed November 12, 2020. https://www.neworleans.com/things-to-do/history/history-of-new -orleans-by-period/.

"Indigenous Tribes of New Orleans and Louisiana." American Library Association, accessed November 12, 2020. http://www.ala.org/aboutala /offices/nola-tribes.

Hinnant, Lori. "How a 2012 Attack Ushered in an Era of Terror for France." Associated Press, October 1, 2017. https://apnews.com/article /0d8ad50b61e04e698149083c003d84ec.

Musodza, Masimba. "The Ties That Bind: Reggae, Rastafari, Judaism and Israel." *Times of Israel*, November 20, 2015. https://blogs.timesofisrael .com/the-ties-that-bind-reggae-rastafari-judaism-and-israel/.

Roth, Matthue. "When Nina Simone Sang a Zionist Standard." Jewish Telegraphic Agency, accessed November 12, 2020. https://www.jta.org /jewniverse/2015/when-nina-simone-sang-a-zionist-standard.

"Religion in Louisiana." Best Places, accessed December 4, 2020. https://www
.bestplaces.net/religion/state/louisiana.

"Religious Composition of Adults in Louisiana." Pew Research Center,
accessed November 12, 2020. https://www.pewforum.org/religious
-landscape-study/state/louisiana/.

"Home." Theory of Enchantment, accessed November 12, 2020. https://
theoryofenchantment.com.

Chapter 8

"Auschwitz: How Death Camp Became Centre of Nazi Holocaust." BBC
News, January 23, 2020. https://www.bbc.com/news/world-europe
-50743973.

Al Jazeera. "Bosnia 1992: The Omarska Camp." May 10, 2017.
https://www.aljazeera.com/program/al-jazeera-world/2017/5/10
/bosnia-1992-the-omarska-camp/.

"Chapel of the Miraculous Image of the Merciful Jesus and the Tomb of
St. Faustina." The Congregation of the Sisters of Our Lady of Mercy,
accessed November 12, 2020. https://www.saint-faustina.org/chapel
-of-the-miraculous-image-of-the-merciful-jesus-and-the-tomb-of-st
-faustina/.

Desbois, Father Patrick. *The Holocaust by Bullets: A Priest's Journey to Uncover
the Truth behind the Murder of 1.5 Million Jews.* New York: St. Martin's
Griffin, 2009.

Scaturro, Michael. "Ukraine Remembers Nazis' Jewish Victims." DW, July 6,
2017. https://www.dw.com/en/ukraine-remembers-nazis-jewish-victims
/a-18563460.

Al Jazeera. "Six Years on, Yazidis in Iraq Demand Justice for ISIL Persecution."
August 4, 2020. https://www.aljazeera.com/news/2020/8/4/six-years-on
-yazidis-in-iraq-demand-justice-for-isil-persecution.

"The Map of Holocaust by Bullets." Yahad-In Unum, accessed November 12, 2020. https://yahadmap.org/#map/.

Washington Post. "Opinion: Ukraine's Part in the Holocaust." May 31, 2019. https://www.washingtonpost.com/opinions/ukraines-part-in-the-holocaust/2019/05/31/9922ad8e-8259-11e9-b585-e36b16a531aa_story.html.

Epilogue
Dervishi, Kay. "Why Have Anti-Semitic Hate Crimes Risen in New York?" City & State New York, January 29, 2020. https://www.cityandstateny.com/articles/politics/ask-experts/why-have-anti-semitic-risen-new-york.html.